# THE COSMIC HARP

APOLLO THE PATRON OF MUSIC

# THE COSMIC HARP

*By*

CORINNE HELINE

*1969*

J. F. ROWNY PRESS, *Publishers*
Santa Barbara
Calif.

*Printed in The United States of America*

# INTRODUCTION

The whole solar system is one vast musical instrument, spoken of in Greek mythology as "the seven-stringed lyre of Apollo." The signs of the Zodiac may be said to be the sounding board of the cosmic harp and the seven planets are the strings; they emit different sounds as they pass through the various signs, and therefore they influence mankind in diverse manner. Should the harmony fail for one single moment, should there be the slightest discord in the heavenly band, the whole universe as such must crumble. —*Max Heindel*

Astronomers define the Zodiac as a wide belt of stars which forms a complete circle around the sky. It is within this circle of the Zodiac that the Sun, Moon and planets are found. The famed Greek astronomer-poet Aratus poetically described the Zodiac in the following lines:

> The Man who held the Watering Pot,
> The Ram, the Bull, the Heavenly Twins;
> And next the Crab the Lion shine.
> The Virgin and the Scales,
> The Scorpion, Archer and Sea-Goat—
> And Fishes with glittering tails.

Esotericists understand the Zodiac to be composed of twelve divine Hierarchies whose magnificence and power are beyond all description. These mighty Beings guide the physical, mental and spiritual evolution of the human race.

> *I have never written the music that was in my heart to write; perhaps I never shall with this brain and these fingers, but I know that hereafter it will be written: when, instead of these few inlets of the senses through which we now secure impressions from without, there shall be a flood of impressions from all sides; and instead of these few tones of our little octave there shall be an infinite scale of harmonies — for I feel it, I am sure of it. This world of music, whose borders even now I have scarcely entered, is a reality, is immortal.*
>
> MOZART

# TABLE OF CONTENTS


| | | |
|---|---|---|
| Dedication | | v |
| Introduction | | vii |
| *Chapter* | | *Page* |
| I | ARIES—*Xeophim* | 11 |
| II | TAURUS—*Tetraphim* | 20 |
| III | GEMINI—*Seraphim* | 25 |
| IV | CANCER—*Cherubim* | 40 |
| V | LEO—*The Lords of Flame* | 46 |
| VI | VIRGO—*The Lords of Wisdom* | 52 |
| VII | LIBRA—*The Lords of Individuality* | 56 |
| VIII | SCORPIO—*The Lords of Form* | 61 |
| IX | SAGITTARIUS—*The Lords of Mind* | 67 |
| X | CAPRICORN—*The Archangels* | 73 |
| XI | AQUARIUS—*The Angels* | 79 |
| XII | PISCES—*Virgin Spirits* | 88 |

# *Chapter I*

## ARIES—Xeophim

THE HIERARCHY of Aries holds the cosmic pattern of perfected God-man or, in modern terminology, Christed man. Each individual, from the lowest to the highest, continuously undergoes gradual and progressive development. The sublime Hierarchy of Aries has now attained to the status where its only contact is with the highest realm of this earth planet, described in western esotericism as the World of God. Hence, its teaching is passed down to its opposite sign, the Hierarchy of Libra Lords of Individuality which is working to help man unfold the latent divinity within himself.

The work of Aries is accomplished under its own musical Ray attuned to its own particular keynote. Characteristic Arian music is martial in rhythm. This does not mean, however, the type of music that inspires such love of one's own country as generates aversion to so-called enemy nations. The highest message of Arian music is a call to the Great Overcoming, the conquest of personality by spirit or the attainment of spiritual rather than material goals.

Historical records of the most primitive races evidence their knowledge of the Zodiac. From the dawn of civilization figures depicting zodiacal signs have been used as decorative motifs for Temples, palaces and public meeting places. Earliest humanity had the faculty of clairvoyance as a common heritage. The people were thus able to see sublime Beings and to observe their activities. Hence those Beings were looked upon as gods and were endowed with both supernatural and magical attributes. This was the basis for the mythology of the ancients, the myths being sacred Temple teachings communicated to the masses in veiled terminology and symbols.

All religions have had an inner and an outer teaching. A beautiful mythological version connected with the Arian Hierarchy is the one known as *The Golden Fleece.* As it sped with the fleetness of wind over land and sea, the Ram which possessed this golden fleece was made radiant by its luminous aura. The trials which beset the Greek hero Jason and his followers when they sought to find and capture the shining Ram are a veiled description of a disciple's efforts to create his Golden Wedding Garment whereby he can travel with the speed of light.

Another illuminating legend connected with Aries is the one about the Phoenix, a bird whose feathers radiate all the colors of the rainbow. Each year, on the day the Sun enters the sign Aries, this exquisite creature builds its own funeral pyre. Then, to the accompaniment of celestial music, its body is consumed by the flames and from the ashes arises a more magnificent Phoenix Bird. This is a fanciful description of the reincarnational cycles of the human spirit. In accordance with divine law and order, from the old must be born the new on an ever ascending spiral toward perfection.

When educators have learned more about the psychological effects of music they will give it a more prominent part in school curriculums than it now has. As office workers are permitted "coffee breaks" during working hours, school children will have musical interludes for the same purpose of physical and mental relaxation. The music of Bach will splendidly serve this purpose: his simple fugues and organ numbers for young children; his symphonies and cantatas for older pupils.

If either adults or children are suffering from extreme emotional tension, the symphonies of Haydn have a beneficial effect, especially if played softly and not too close to the patient. When Aries natives are engaged in such advanced spiritual work as transmutation or higher degrees of meditation like contemplation and adoration, the Passion music of Bach and Haydn's *Creation* will be most helpful.

The musical keynote of Aries is B flat major. Compositions

written in this key should be physically and mentally stimulating and inspiring to the Aries native.

Aries is the first sign of the Zodiac, a power sign. The Aries native looks out over the world, so to speak; it is a new realm which is his to conquer if he will. Hence, pioneering, adventure and daring are known as the keywords of Aries. Natives of this sign hew out their own way, usually alone and unaided.

An annual flow of Arian power floods the earth at the beginning of the spiritual New Year, the Eastertide of resurrected life. The high significance of this sign is found, therefore, in sacrifice and transmutation. These may be summed up as self-control, the supreme goal of the awakened Arian natives. Intellect must merge with wisdom and self-consciousness must be sublimated into Christ consciousness before they come into full possession of their power.

## Johann Sebastian Bach — 1685-1750

Johann Sebastian Bach was unquestionably one of the highest channels for the inflow of true spiritual music that the world has ever known. Realizing at an early age his own remarkable musical abilities, in a spirit of reverence and humility he dedicated himself and his divine art to God. To this dedication he remained steadfast throughout his entire life.

The independence of the Arian nature, and its ability to make its way alone, were paramount in Bach's make-up from his early youth. His destiny was so clear to him, and his genius so compelling, that what would seem like obstacles to others became incentives to Bach. Before he was twenty-two years of age this composer-musician held an important position as organist at Weimar, where he renewed his determination to devote his music to the service and glory of the Most High. The beautiful old cathedral with its soft lights, rose windows, stalls of rare medieval workmanship and rich tapestries made a fitting shrine for young Bach's devout spirit and flaming genius. His work during the Weimar years placed him among the immortals. He produced fifty Cantatas, two Passions which are still unrivalled, and a Magnificat that is equally unique, standing alone in its class.

Bach was born on March 21st, 1685, in Eisenach, a village dowered with rare beauty, while religion, romance and music charged its atmosphere with poetry. The little town was overshadowed by the great castle of Wartburg, made famous by the minnesingers and its use as the locale of Wagner's *Tannhauser*. If it be true that an advanced ego chooses its own birthplace, Bach could not have selected one more fitting to his temperament and genius.

Johann Sebastian came of a long line of musical ancestors, the name of Bach being an illustrious one in the musical annals of Germany. Johann, however, was the first to consecrate his talent entirely to religion. This preference was evident when, as a lad of eight, he entered school and his favorite studies were the Psalms, the Gospels and the Epistles, which he learned verbatim in both German and Latin. This spiritual predilection was unfaltering. Years later he was teaching his own children to invoke the name of Jesus before playing five-finger exercises.

Bach evidenced the alert mentality so typical of Aries, and was always registered in classes with boys several years his senior. On Easter Sunday, April 3rd, 1700, the lad was enrolled as a choir boy in one of the many imposing churches of Luneburg. Again the atmosphere and environment of this quaint village was most harmonious with his temperament and most conducive to his further spiritual development. "Topping every building in lavish altitude, three great churches, impressive monuments of ancient piety, declare the city's heirship of the Age of Faith." A cloistered peace pervaded the whole place. And here it was that the genius of the youthful musician began its flowering.

The *Chorus Symphonicus,* with which Bach was affiliated, functioned on Sundays and with special obligations for the holy seasonal festivals. In Bach's time materiality had not made such encroachments upon human minds as it has in this modern day.

Men were still sufficiently sensitized to receive something of the powerful spiritual inflow released to earth during those periods. No doubt this rarely gifted composer, who lived always in close attunement with nature, received at these periods much of the inspiration that he expressed later in his immortal music — for such is the influence of the inflow at Christmas, Easter, and the Feasts of St. John the Baptist (Midsummer Eve) and St. Michael the Archangel (Michaelmas). His early Fugues and Chorals are redolent with praise and homage to the Lord Christ Jesus, while many of his Cantatas were composed for the sacred seasonal festivals and were performed for the first time on those occasions.

The enormity of Bach's musical output reflects the tireless activity of this Arian native. When asked in later years to define the secret of his attainment, his reply contained two Aries keywords: *unceasing activity* and *self-control.* "The successful master," he added, "must have submitted himself to the discipline of self-instruction before he can hope to meet and overcome the difficulties of others."

On Good Friday, 1729, Bach produced the last and greatest of his Passions, *St. Matthew's Passion,* which has been acclaimed "the most notable and inspired treatment of its subject in the entire range of music." This work is also indicative of the composer's profound understanding of and reverence for the Holy Scriptures.

Aries rules the head. So it is in accordance with his astrological rulership that Bach's music is mental rather than emotional. It is of a quality that makes for strengthening, purifying and spiritualizing the mind.

Bach's color-tone is the clear blue of a gas flame — the color of the Father principle which, like Aries, is positive and creative.

When the time for his transition came, this master musician was working assiduously on a Choral in homage to the Lord, his own spirit in attunement with the lines that his glorious music has immortalized:

*Grant that my end may worthy be*
*And that I may wake thy face to see.*

His passing was fittingly announced in the statement "He has passed to his rest and now sleeps blessedly in God."

## Joseph Haydn — 1732-1809

Independence and self-reliance, together with eagerness for treading new and untried paths so characteristic of Aries, were fully manifested in the life and career of Joseph Haydn, born March 31st, 1732. At the tender age of five he was literally "on his own" because of the extreme poverty of a large and rapidly increasing family. Joseph was apprenticed to an uncle who agreed to give musical instruction in payment for the boy's manual labor. Although the work was heavy and the hours long for so young a child, the Sun, which keeps alight the optimistic fire of Aries, continued to shine for Joseph. He never lost his cheerful and enthusiastic demeanor. Years later, when the laurel of immortal fame had crowned his brow, he returned to visit the humble home of his youth and reverently kissed its doorstep in gratitude for the training that made possible his musical career.

Biographers comment upon the extremely warm and cordial friendship that existed between Haydn and Mozart, although the former was older by twenty years. Students of star lore are particularly interested in the astral delineation of their character differences. The older composer was fascinated by the quick-silver personality of Piscean Mozart while the younger was equally charmed by the steadfastness and warmth so natural to the fiery Arian Haydn.

Any artist who attains the creative status that was Haydn's becomes a very responsive channel for the expression of contemporary trends. For this reason the history of a nation and its people may be interpreted by their music. About the middle of the eighteenth century romantic sentiment predominated to the extent that this sentiment bade fair to supersede intellect as the motivating force of the period. The music of Haydn is imbued with its rich and deepening influence, the emotions of love, melancholy and grief finding a most adequate expression in his music for stringed instruments.

Haydn's work for strings is unexcelled to this day. He has been dubbed the "Father of the Symphony." In perfect attunement with Arian tendencies, Haydn was interested in everything new. He was, therefore, in sympathy with the rising romantic school of music—wherein young Beethoven was destined to shine so brilliantly.

It has been said of Haydn that he was forever playing some instrument, and that he thought in terms of instruments even when writing for voices. His tireless genius gave to the world thirty or more symphonies, an equal number of string quartet compositions and much chamber music. This great classical master also produced some magnificent church music in his Masses. His crowning achievements were, however, his two Oratorios: *The Creation* and *The Seasons.* It was his custom to place the words *Laus Deo* at the end of each and every composition.

The Aries urge to new modes of expression led Haydn into writing Oratorios. The idea for one of his masterpieces, *The Creation,* was inspired by a friend's giving him a Bible and saying, "Begin there at the beginning." The years he devoted to the composition of this glorious Oratorio were the most satisfying of Haydn's whole life. He himself wrote, "When working on The Creation I knelt every day and prayed to God to strengthen me for my work." And again: "When I think of God, I can only conceive of Him as a Being infinitely great and infinitely good. This last quality of the divine nature inspires me with such confidence and joy that I could have written a *miserere* in *tempo allegro.*" These are the expressions of a true Aries, Aries the irrepressible, the supremely confident, the translator of misery into joy, of death into life.

In the magnificent *Chaos* overture of *The Creation* Haydn demonstrates the universality, breadth of vision and divine oneness of the All; and this is the prerogative and the highest expression of music. This overture has been styled "the crown on a god's head." In its transcendent climax, "*And there was light,*" the music changes from innerplane harmonies sounded in C minor to outer-world activities expressed in C major.

Following the completion of *The Creation* in 1789, Haydn devoted the next three years to his second great Oratorio, *The Seasons.* In lieu of a detailed analysis of this work, we add simply that the inspired master drew down key-tones of vast cosmic harmonies that accompany seasonal changes in nature. In the New Age renaissance this Oratorio will be used to further the spiritual development of humanity.

In a volume entitled *Haydn,* Karl Geiringer states: "Always experimenting and trying out new devices, always eager to improve, never clinging to tradition, these qualities enabled Haydn at the age of nearly seventy to write the great Oratorios that marked the climax of his creative output.

"Haydn was entirely unprejudiced. He was equally receptive to influences from great and small sources, from north, south or west. He could afford to study and follow new methods for he was entirely sure of himself. Haydn, in body and mind one of the healthiest of all composers, knew that whatever he tried the firm, gentle, humorous, eternally young, optimistic core of his personality would remain unchanged."

## SERGEI V. RACHMANINOFF — 1873-1943

Sergei V. Rachmaninoff, one of the most popular of modern composers, was born April 1, 1873, and left this earth plane March 28, 1943. He also showed remarkable musical talent at an early age.

Perhaps the supreme inspiration of his life was his fellow countryman, Peter Tchaikovsky, Russia's great musical genius. When only thirteen years of age, Rachmaninoff made a piano arrangement of Tchaikovsky's *Manfred* which so pleased the master that ever afterwards he showed marked interest in the younger musician's career and assisted him in every possible way.

Rachmaninoff manifested true Arian activity and inspiration

in productivity and composition. His published works include numerous songs as well as piano pieces for both two and four hands. His *Prelude in C Sharp Minor* was his first composition to bring him international repute. Two operas, *Aleko* and *Francesca de Rimini,* have been produced with considerable success. *The Island of the Dead,* a wierd, bizarre, compelling fragment and his most famous symphonic poem, was "brought through" from past memories.

Rachmaninoff's color note is clear green-gold. His music is conducive to the development of logical and well-balanced thinking. A boy or girl with "scatter brain" tendencies relative to study will benefit greatly by using this composer's music during regular study periods.

# Chapter II

## TAURUS—Tetraphim

THE CONSTELLATION of Taurus, the Bull, is one of the most magnificent in the heavens due to its own bright stars and to the close proximity of some of the most brilliant lights of the sky. Across the head of the Bull shines the Hyades, sometimes termed "the misty daughters of the sky." The central figure of this cluster is Alderbaran, a wonderful golden star of the first magnitude which glitters like a priceless jewel in the "eye" of the Bull. At the tip of one of its horns gleams Elnath, appropriately described as "the budding one," while not far distant shines Orion, the mighty hunter.

Beginning about 4000 B.C., the Sun passed by precession through the sign Taurus. During this journey worship of the Bull predominated throughout many lands. Excavation of Assyrian, Babylonian and Persian monuments and coins bears witness to this fact; and even today cows are considered sacred in India. Ruins found in the ancient Egyptian city of Memphis evidence the magnificence of Temples dedicated to this worship. The same is true of two stately mausoleums where funeral ceremonials were performed with the pomp and honor accorded only to heroes. It is probable that these early races retained some memory of the glorious celestial Beings who compose the Hierarchy of Taurus. Hence, its prototype in the heavens appeared to them to have the form of a bull, so this animal was chosen as an object of worship.

The sublime Hierarchy of Taurus holds the Cosmic Pattern of *form* for the earth planet. Like the Hierarchy of Aries, the Taurean Hierarchy has progressed so far in spiritual attainment that it contacts only the highest sphere of our system, the

World of God. Therefore, its work has also been passed down to the opposite sign Scorpio; the Lords of Form. The latter are continuing the work of Taurus, as every living thing must possess a physical vehicle in order to progress on this physical plane.

Scorpio governs the month of November while Taurus rules the month of May. It is significant to note that the most ancient of primitive races observed two principal festivities: one, dedicated to the dead, was at the beginning of November; the other, the festival of resurrection, was at the beginning of May. Even in the Christian church of today the first day of November is All Saints Day when prayers are said for the dead. Among early-day Aztecs a human being was sacrificed at the November feast to propitiate the God of Death that he might bestow added blessings on the living. These two annual observances are related to the seasonal changes. By November the earth has passed completely out of the light and gladness of summer into the darkness and gloom of winter. By May the winter's death-like sleep is exchanged for resurrected life.

The observances, however, find their true origin in Temple teachings given to man at the beginning of his earthly sojourn. The mystic key to Initiation is the overcoming of transient death by life eternal. Scorpio is the sign of death; but it is also the sign of transmutation. When St. Paul came to understand this truth through Initiation (Illumination), he gave forth an exultant song of the spirit: "O death, where is thy sting? O grave, where is thy victory?"

The musical keynote of Taurus, a sign of beauty and harmony, is E flat major. The music which gives refreshment and renewal to the Taurean native is that wherein these qualities are expressed, as in the two Strauss waltzes, *The Blue Danube* and *Tales of the Vienna Woods,* also the exquisitely beautiful Tchaikovsky ballet music. That composer's symphonies, especially the *F minor Number Four* and the *B minor Number Six* are ideal for a Taurean's deep meditation and concentration.

## PETER ILICH TCHAIKOVSKY — 1840-1893

Sometime in the future we shall be wise enough to study the history of various nations from the viewpoint of both inner and outer plane occurrences. We shall then know how worldly events are spiritually determined; and how the Lords of Destiny send Master Egos into incarnation at precise historical moments, racial settings and geographical locations that they may perform important missions according to their special genius.

Such an ego Peter Ilich Tchaikovsky, greatest of all Russian master-musicians, born May 7, 1840, under the sign Taurus, the home of Venus, Goddess of Love and bearer of beauty. Working through the harmonizing power of this celestial sign, the composer gave to his people music that served as a cohesive, integrating force during the period of his lifetime and later, when destructive revolutionary energies might have swept the nation off her destined path. Artistically, Russia was practically barren at the time of Tchaikovsky's birth, but stirring within the people was an aspiration for the liberty, equality and social justice that are their rightful heritage under New Age Aquarian rulership. It is clear that this was not to be realized short of the vast upheavals which Uranus, ruler of Aquarius, brings in its train when it enters upon the scene to make all things new. So great was the foreseen social revolt that steps were taken by the Wise Ones to counteract it lest events should terminate in general ruin.

Music is such a force, and Tchaikovsky became a messenger for its needed release in the life of this young and growing nation. So conscious was he that his mission was essentially Russian that he would not have it said there were Polish strains in his ancestry, but proudly insisted that he was "entirely Russian." Early in life he became aware of his great calling and began improvising and composing while a mere child. He claimed Mozart as his supreme inspiration. As a young lad, listening to this composer's music he would hold his head and cry out ecstatically, "Oh the music, it's here and won't let me rest." Later he referred to Mozart as having opened the door for him into another world where exquisite sound predominated.

Under the tutelage of Rubenstein, founder of the St. Petersburg Conservatory of Music, the budding genius of Tchaikovsky came into its full flowering. At the age of twenty-three his way had become clear and his mission sure. Then as a result of his brilliant work at the Conservatory of Moscow, he won acclaim as the brightest musical star in the Russian firmament and the nation's truest musical servant. All the sorrow and melancholy, all the pain and tears that Russia has known, and must yet know before she finds her real self, are expressed in the music of her Race Spirit. Tchaikovsky is the voice of that Spirit. His music may be likened to the falling of amber (his color note) tears on a crushed and broken heart.

*None but the Lonely Heart,* the most popular of Tchaikovsky's songs, typifies this nation-wide sadness and the inevitableness of Russian suffering. Having been an inspired channel almost from the beginning of his life, he once wrote: "My works pour through me so easily and simply, some I write practically at one sitting." His *Swan Lake,* a marvellously descriptive expression of the magic and beauty of early, half-legendary Russia, has been termed the foundation upon which Russia's supreme art form, the ballet, was built.

Taurus, an earth sign, is the home of Venusian beauty. These two influences enable taurean natives to tune in to the beauties of nature. In Tchaikovsky's case this attunement found expression in what is termed "nature music." Cyril Scott, in his occult study of music, places this composer with Grieg as the two most gifted forerunners of Deva music, that later found transcription through such exponents as Ravel, Debussy and, above all, Scriabin.

One of Tchaikovsky's most important compositions and, it is said, his own favorite, is the *Fourth Symphony.* In it the implacability of the Fate theme is indicative of Russia's past and present tragic state, while the half-whimsical and hauntingly lovely Dream motif belongs to the Russia of the future. In its totality the symphony sounds forth unity, harmony and beauty, the principal keynotes of Taurus and the basic musical structure whereon the New Russia will be founded.

Little do the people of our day realize how great is the role of music in the rise and fall of nations and in the evolutionary processes relative to man and nature. One of the objectives of this volume is to further that realization by stressing the cosmic aspect of the link between a composer and his zodiacal ruler, thus revealing the type of energy he is releasing into the evolutionary stream.

# Chapter III

## GEMINI—Seraphim

THE TWIN STARS of Gemini are easily discernable as they are the two brightest stars in the northern hemisphere and are always seen together. Pollux, the more brilliant of the two, is a star of the first magnitude, while Castor is a star of the second magnitude. An ancient legend relates that the twins were once human beings, brothers of the beautiful Helen of Troy over whom the Trojan war was fought. One of the brothers was mortally wounded. The other, in anguish and despair, pleaded with Jupiter, king of the gods, to let his brother return to mortal life or permit them to be reunited in the nether world. Because of their great love for one another, Jupiter took pity on them and placed them together in the sky as twin stars, decreeing they never again should be parted.

Another Greek legend tells how Jason and his followers set forth in quest of the golden fleece. A violent storm overtook the voyagers and their ship was all but dashed to pieces when Orpheus came to their rescue. The God of Music played upon his magic lute until the towering waves subsided and the clouds overhead disappeared. Shining in the calm blue heavens above were Castor and Pollux, as though bestowing a blessing on the adventurers. Thenceforth the twin stars have been looked upon as patron saints of the sea and of all seafarers. A poet thus describes their protection:

*Safe comes the ship to haven,*
*Through billows and through gales—*
*If once the great Twin Brothers*
*Sit shining on the sails.*

The Hierarchy of Gemini bears the name of the Seraphim. Like the two preceding Hierarchies, Aries and Taurus, the Lords of Gemini have passed into "liberation" from earthly assignments. They only contact this planet through its second highest spiritual realm, the World of Virgin Spirits. The Seraphim have passed their work down to Sagittarius, the Lords of Mind and Gemini's opposite sign.

The work of the Seraphim is to unite life with form. The Hierarchy of Gemini is very important in the life of humanity because it governs *polarity,* the very foundation of life itself and of occult philosophy. Polarity is the perfect equalization of the masculine and feminine principles within man's body, and will be the attainment of the human race by the end of the Earth Period. Then the Seraphim will be the teachers and guardians of all who reach this exalted status. Therefore they hold the Cosmic Pattern of the androgyne body, the perfected vehicle of those who attain polarity.

In the light of this knowledge it is interesting to note that the oldest Chinese civilization acknowledged a dual Godhead to which they attributed all harmonious relationships that existed between heaven and earth. Yang was the masculine principle manifested by the Sun, which ruled summer and life. Yin was the feminine principle manifested by the Moon, which governed winter and death. Chinese religion and folklore were based on the interaction between these two principles, and it possessed what is estimated as the oldest symbol of polarity ever given to man: a perfect circle formed of two integrated halves, one white and the other black. Their ancient teaching on polarity was no doubt given to them by Atlantean priests who migrated to China and became the first teachers of men following the Great Flood which destroyed the continent of Atlantis.

The musical keynote of Gemini is F sharp major. A Gemini native will receive much refreshment and inspiration from compositions written in this key, such as Edvard Grieg's lovely *Spring Song.* The Gemini individual is restless, ever seeking and searching for something higher. To be of the greatest benefit to them, music must be of the type that lifts one above the stress, noise and confusion of the outer realm and relates him to the peace, quiet and order of the divine realm within himself. Cardinal Newman's beautiful *Lead Kindly Light* and the familiar hymn *Abide with Me* are ideal. Richard Wagner's *Evening Star* from *Tannhauser* and *Elsa's Prayer* from *Lohengrin* are suggested for a Gemini's periods of contemplation and meditation. An aid in lifting his consciousness above the objective plane and putting him in attunement with the divine subjective will be found in *Solveig's Song* from Greig's *Peer Gynt Suite,* and in Marguerite's *Exaltation Song* from Gounod's *Faust*. The latter is heard in the final act of the opera wherein Marguerite makes the momentous decision that brings about her redemption and triumphant translation.

## RICHARD WAGNER — 1813-1883

We have said that Gemini, sign of the Twins, is dual in nature. This duality is also represented by two upright columns, one black and the other white. Since Gemini is an airy mental sign ruled by Mercury, the two columns symbolize the human mind, the black column indicating the purely human mind; the white one, the regenerated or Christed mind.

In Richard Wagner this duality was so pronounced that volumes have been written in an attempt to explain the opposites that swayed his passionately human but divinely inspired personality. Without an understanding of the profound aspects of spiritual law under the Hierarchy of Gemini, a nature like that of Wagner's cannot be accurately interpreted.

By virtue of the soul powers he had developed in previous lives (the white column), Wagner became an instrument for channelling into this world a spiritual impulse from the heaven worlds despite the fact he still retained unliquidated liabilities and unregenerated elements in his personal nature (the black column). When his life is studied in the light of his Gemini rulership, it becomes clear how his creative genius could flower so magnificently in spite of the handicaps he had to surmount. His was a titanic struggle against frailties of the flesh, weaknesses of personality, lack of material substance, misunderstandings, persecution and frustration in addition to a period of exile from his homeland.

It is the office of the dual Gemini to link heaven and earth, spirit and form. Under its celestial influence Wagner brought music, the language of the heaven worlds, to the earth plane in a more sustained and tangible form than has been given by any other composer before or since his time. He created the dual art form of music-dramas. These are quite distinct from opera as we know it in that they so combine music with drama they become an integrated unit for expressing any theme whatever. Wagner recognized two sublime artists: Shakespeare and Beethoven. Shakespeare conveyed by word what Beethoven could not communicate through music alone; and conversely, Beethoven transmitted intimations of immortal realities by means of tone that Shakespeare's poetry failed to express. Under his Gemini rulership, Wagner accepted it as his mission to create music-dramas wherein the most glorious of Beethoven's music and of Shakespeare's dramas would be blended into a composite art form. This he did to a degree that places him among the foremost innovators and cultural giants of all time.

There is yet another duality in the nature of Wagner. He is almost as much Taurus as he is Gemini. Born May 22nd, his Sun is in the first degree of Gemini, a cuspal position of Taurus-Gemini. Mercury rules the latter and Venus the former of these two signs. As Mercury governs the spoken word while Venus rules beauty in all its aspects, concrete or abstract, herein lie the powers that inspired Wagner's creation of music-dramas. True to his Taurus-Gemini nativity, Wagner had a kaleidoscopic personality. He was grave and gay, melancholy and buoyant by turns. He could be vehement, eager and intense or compassionate, tender and unpredictable—all characteristics that found expression in his music.

The focus of Wagner's consciousness shifted swiftly between this world of material concerns and the world of spiritual realities. He was never free for long from the battle for the bare necessities of existence or from a need to maintain his social relations and obligations in proper order. But no matter how dark or difficult the situation wherein he frequently found himself, his dynamic spirit enabled him to rise triumphant over every obstacle so he might pursue his creative labors on levels where harmony prevailed.

What has been regarded as Wagner's inordinate vanity and colossal egotism was actually an inner assurance that this was a divine destiny, a preordained career. He was so convinced it was his assigned task to do what he did that nothing in heaven or on earth could prevent its successful culmination. Many of those who worked with him during the dark days of his obscurity and seeming defeat have declared they even then recognized that he had something to sustain him which they lacked. It seems there was a "faint splendor" about him which they regarded as "something almost unapproachable."

How well Wagner came to know "There's a divinity that shapes our ends,/Rough-hew them how we will!" For instance, in the earlier years of his career he set out for Paris with what he believed to be a meritorious work that would capture the city's acclaim. Fate intervened, causing him to pass through stormy seas amid Norwegian reefs. During the voyage he heard the tempestuous song of unbridled waters, and became aware, as never before, of the infinite music within his own soul awaiting expression. There came to him intimations of the fact that he was to become an inspired instrument for a new music which would "sweep over all the old restricting forms like a sea over little artificial water works."

Taurus, sign of beauty and harmony, exercised so dominant an influence over Wagner that it brought into his life the occult powers of Scorpio, polar opposite of Taurus. The deep, strong, mysterious psychic forces released through Scorpio enabled him to immortalize in *The Flying Dutchman,* his first notable work, the song of the sea — which, he declared, he would accomplish in a "new, wild and soul-stirring way." The remote wilderness of the Norwegian cliffs, the overpowering darkness of night at sea, the raging voice of a storm, the anguished cry of the dark

Wanderer, together with the high note of redemption by love, were the mysterious themes that began to take form. This whole music-drama unveils the deep primitive urges, the tempestuous passions and the emotional intensities of sorrow, pain and death. Throughout the work move the forces, both high and low, emanating from the mystic and mysterious sign of Scorpio. Writing about this work at a later date, Wagner stated that "wherever and however I touched my material I trembled with ardor and fire. I always drank at one breath the peculiar aroma which had intoxicated me at its very first conception."

*Tannhauser* was his next creation. A new and even greater light dawned upon his enchanted horizon. Venus, the alluring figure of sensual desire, appeared in contrast to the fair Elizabeth, embodiment of love in its highest and noblest form. Each had graces of a kind which were to be chanted by rival contestants in a festival of song. Upon this ecstatic vision he went to work. This it was which brightened the last of the chill, disappointing days of his early questing in Paris.

As he was journeying back to Leipzig he was uncomfortably wedged in among tradesmen on their way to the city fair, yet he continued to dream of his drama-in-the-making. Then, through the blurred windows of the stage coach, he caught glimpses of the Wartburg Castle and the path that led to its heights from the valley below. In his mind's eye he saw an autumn twilight and an evening star. Now he heard a song to the accompaniment of a harp. This was the song that was to become one of the most inspired arias in *Tannhauser*. Not until the vision had been impressed upon his consciousness was he brought back to earth by the jolting of the coach and the grumbling of fellow passengers. It was Taurean inspiration and it came to flower in *Tannhauser,* for which Venus, Goddess of Love, furnished the leit-motif. Venus, the evening star, gave to Wagner the aria that bears her name.

Time passed and as the young composer pondered over the poetic legends of his native land, a greater music than he had yet composed possessed him. The glorious picture of a knight in white and silver moved before his enraptured vision and he became enveloped in the golden radiance of the Grail. The pure and shining knight hovered halfway between the miraculous and the real in his responsive heart, and from this vision sprang the music-drama of *Lohengrin.* As *The Flying Dutchman* symbolizes the Scorpio influence and *Tannhauser,* with its song of the evening star, reveals the Taurus inspiration, so the tragedy of *Lohengrin* marks Gemini's path toward equilibrium where opposites on lower levels are transformed into complementaries on higher levels. Beyond the degree of equilibrium as portrayed in *Lohengrin* is the perfect fusion of the masculine and feminine principles into one. This degree Wagner portrayed in *Tristan and Isolde,* the music-drama of preparation for the Rite of the Mystic Marriage.

From boyhood Wagner possessed an all-absorbing desire for freedom, "The battle of mankind against existing society has begun," said he. "This battle is the noblest and the holiest one that was ever fought." Out of his dreams of freedom and equality – in pursuit of which he suffered loss of position, imprisonment and exile – he fashioned his glorious proclamation of freedom in *The Ring Cycle.* One of the characters in this cycle of four dramas is Siegfried, who typifies the New Age pioneer who points the way to emancipation into a free, glad world. Regarding him, Wagner wrote: "I shall create and awaken him, make him wander and laugh and *love* in forest and over mountain height, the free, strong, beautiful man who knew no fear."

The theatre of Wagner's day, like the theatre of today, was usually regarded as a place of entertainment only. There was very little recognition of the institution as a temple of art, which Wagner sought to make it. He saw it fulfill its true, high purpose of uplifting and ennobling people and, through bonds of beauty, bringing men "into one vast brotherhood about the altars of true and holy art." This vision inspired the building at Beyreuth of a theatre dedicated solely to the performance of his works. Had Wagner lived to guide this institution along the lines he indicated, it would have become the world's foremost Temple of Art for imparting to those who are duly prepared spiritual experiences of an initiatory character. While it falls short of the ideal set for it, the Beyreuth theatre is a first step toward the restoration of the Mystery Temple of old.

Specially composed for such an institution was *Parsifal,* his last and grandest creation. This consecrational music-drama, as he called it, was to be performed only in a sacred temple. He specifically requested that it was not to be given anywhere but in his theatre at Beyreuth, for Wagner well knew he had brought down the music of angelic realms for the healing and regeneration of those who would attune their lives to its supernal rhythms, the highest ever granted to human hearing.

Despite the incomparable contribution he made to the arts of drama and music, Wagner's mission seems by human reckoning to be but half done. He envisioned and longed to do so much more. Appropriate to him are the appellations "soaring Eagle" and "restless Star." Though persecuted, misunderstood and ridiculed, his valiant spirit remained true to the vision of a New Day and a redeemed humanity, and toward their realization he consecrated the whole vast range of his creative genius. Perhaps the world of tomorow will be able to estimate rightly the debt it owes to the pioneering spirit of Wagner.

Mauve, purple and white-gold were his color tones. His music is true Neptunian. Its supreme purpose is to aid man in the unfoldment of his higher nature and the attainment of Illumination.

## CHARLES GOUNOD — 1818-1893

Charles Gounod, the well known French composer, affords an interesting Gemini study in contrasts. One of his early musical instructors said of him, "He finds interest and pleasure in everything, and what I like best, he always wants to know the reason why." This questioning attitude is a marked characteristic of Gemini children.

True to his astrological rulership, Gounod in his autobiography writes: "Steadiness was never my strong point. I fear a weakness uncounterbalanced by good sense may easily become a power for evil." And again, in his definition of art, he gives expression to the highest idealism of his sign: "Art is neither an utter dream nor an exact copy; it is neither a mere ideal nor the merely real. It is like man himself — the meeting and fusion of the two. *It is unity in duality.*" In these words we find the true significance of Gemini, and Gounod lived up to this lofty idealism in his art.

He was born in Paris June 7, 1818, and was determined from childhood that no obstacle should prevent his following a musical career. It was a resolve that was, in very truth, a dedication to the task he had come to perform, a cause he was destined to serve. After making such dedication, strong souls are invariably given trials to test the strength of their resolution. Gounod was no exception to this rule. He encountered both extremes of poverty and parental opposition, but neither proved able to dissuade him from his purposed course. His goal included the Grand Prix de Rome and a chair in the Paris Conservatory, both of which he realized.

It was during his ecstatic rambles on the beautiful Isle of Capri, and in its "phosphorescent nights," as he refers to them, that he found much of his inspiration for his opera *Faust*. Seventeen years later he completed this work which is, perhaps, the one that gave world-wide luster to his name. This opera had its premiere in Paris March 19, 1859, under the supervision of the composer himself.

The drama is keyed to Gemini. It is dual in form, being in two parts, and deals with man's nature in its higher and lower aspects — "two souls housed within our breast that struggle there for undivided reign," as Faust expresses it. In Part I, the character of Faust is a presentation of man as he functions on the lower sense plane. In Part II, Faust is the regenerated man in whom the soul is in control, thus typifying the glory of a redeemed mankind. Relative to the pictorial representation of Gemini, the black and white columns, Part I is the black column while Part II is the white one.

It is also to be noted that the music of *Faust* is Neptunian in its influence upon those who hear it, and that Neptune is the higher octave of Mercury, ruler of Gemini. Gounod wrought better than he knew when he attuned himself to the high Gemini currents that inspire the musical accompaniment to this drama of human emancipation.

Gounod's color-note is a soft misty blue. His music may be used in meditation to produce that divine inner stillness so necessary to one's well-being in this era of speed and confusion.

## EDVARD GRIEG — 1843-1907

Another Gemini quality appears in the music of Edvard Grieg. This composer drew upon two kingdoms in nature, namely, the kingdom of nature spirits and the kingdom of man. His compositions link them into an ever-expanding unity of expression.

The spirit of Norway becomes articulate in the music of Grieg. Norwegian folk music was the prime source of his inspiration. "How strange," he wrote, "is life, like the folk tunes of which one knows not whether they are conceived in major or in minor." He added that when he discovered northern folk music he found at the same time his own life work. While wandering through the valleys of his native land, he heard the strange, almost ethereal songs of the peasants, which gave a distinctive quality to his compositions. And in the silences of the open white spaces he learned to attune himself with the rhythms of nature.

The keynote of elves and brownies sounds in *The Hall of the Mountain King*. The sprites of fire and air are heard in *Anitra's Dance,* while *Solveig's Song* echoes the strains of the Guardian Spirit of Norway's mighty snow crests. The peace and calm that pervaded the composer's home — Troldhaugen, the home of trolls and spirits — was so pronounced and of such high quality that friends declared that Grieg's entire estate seemed to be singing *Solveig's Song*.

To each nation there comes the messenger from the great

inner Temple of Music who is best qualified to be used by that nation's Race Spirit as a channel for furthering the people's evolution by means of music. Bach was such an instrument for Germany. Palestrina was so used in Italy, Chopin in Poland, Tschaikovsky in Russia. In Norway it was Grieg. Through his music, more than through any other single factor, Norway's life, customs and folklore have become familiar the world over.

"Mysterious gloom and indomitable wildness — these are the contrasts of Norwegian folk-song," wrote Grieg. And these are the elements that give character to his music. One critic wrote of his work: "He formed a new kind of music differing from the classical German art as an exotic orchid of the forest differs from the beautiful, but regular, garden flowers."

The exquisite tenderness and soulful quality of Grieg's love songs give them a place beside Schumann at his best. The songs were all inspired by his love for and devotion to Mme. Grieg, with whom he knew many years of perfect companionship. Perhaps the most popular of all his songs is *I Love You,* written for her at the time of their betrothal.

It is significant that, having found himself so completely in Norwegian folk music, Grieg was unable to compose when away from home. He said relative to this fact, "The tone I find good one day, I tear out of my heart the next because they are not genuine." A poet observes that the eyes are the "windows of the soul." The eyes of Grieg have been described as reflecting the blue of Norway's skies and the mystic luminosity of her fjords.

The composer's final resting place is as romantic as his music. A high and steep cliff, plainly visible from his beloved Troldhaugen, projects into a fjord. Near the middle of this fifty-foot precipice is a natural grotto that can be reached by boat only. Grieg chose this spot as his burial place. Here, amidst the quiet and solitude he loved so well, surrounded by nature's white and green, was interred all that was mortal of Edvard Grieg. Born June 15, 1843, his spirit left the earth plane sixty-four years later on September 3, 1907. He belonged to an air sign so was attuned to the element Air, physically, mentally and artistically. It is not strange, therefore, that this son of Gemini chose an elevation reaching toward the sky for his final resting place.

Grieg's music is especially potent in relieving enervation and depletion, particularly of the nervous system.

## Robert Schumann – 1810-1856

Robert Schumann first saw the light of day on June 8, 1810. He was a strange, shy, elusive child who wove bizarre stories of ghosts, fairies and elves to the mystification of other children; and who, at the age of seven, was inscribing these airy fancies into musical compositions that took the form of eerie little dances. His father, noting the unusual talents of his son, dedicated him at that early age to a career of music and art.

The dual characteristics of Gemini set their impress upon the life and music of Schumann. He was a dreamer and a realist, an idealist and a man able to hold his own in the practical field. Throughout his life he was noted for his independence and originality, both of which are Gemini traits. These qualifications often brought him into trouble with his teachers, who regarded him as the most original of pupils as he was later named the most original of composers.

In his youth the pendulum was still swinging between the ideal and the actual. Should he devote himself to music or to law? This question perplexed him as part of his "eternal inner soul struggle." Indecision is another typical Gemini quality. Not without good reason was it asked, "Can Robert really *will* something?" Then it was added, "His disposition is very variable." At this time Schumann himself wrote: "Now I stand at the crossways and am startled at the question – whither?" It was the final and propitious choice that led him to his distinguished career and gave the world some of its loveliest, most soul-stirring music. It also brought him years of perfect comradeship with Clara Wieck, who became his understanding and gifted wife.

When the young composer entered the Wieck household as a pupil of Clara's father, his serious dedication was made to the Muse of both love and music. In his marriage with Clara Schumann he realized the consummation of Gemini: the amalgamation of *duality into unity*. His genius found inspiration in his love. Most of his important work was dedicated to Clara. She, in turn, added to his fame by playing his compositions in her concerts. The couple was styled "the great Schumanns," and Robert's letters to Clara are an index to their perfect mating. On the day of his mother's death he wrote his wife: "Behind all the darkness is your glowing picture and I bear everything more easily." Schumann's exquisite *Traumerei,* whose tender, haunting beauty has won world-wide favor, was a connecting link between the spirits of Robert and Clara Schumann. He wrote it for her and she used it to introduce his genius to the public.

Later, as the rich fruitage of their years together became more and more evident in his music, he wrote: "This music in me now, and always such lovely melodies! Thoughts of you form their chief part and I am going to dedicate them all to you. You will smile so sweetly when you recognize yourself." Again, while she was on a concert tour he wrote: "I often think of you, not as a brother thinks of a sister, nor as a friend thinks of a friend, but rather as a pilgrim thinks of a distant altar piece."

Schumann's sensitive soul and rare intuition evidently recognized Clara as his own while she was a mere child, and he delighted her with his eerie tales of "hidden lands." After their marriage in 1840 he wrote the majority of his exquisitely tender and beautiful songs. Besides these he composed remarkable groups of chamber music, four symphonies and numerous other important orchestral works, all flowing easily and joyously from the inspiration of his life with Clara. He described this period thus: "Concert of the Schumann couple. Happy unforgettable evening. My Clara played everything in such masterly manner and in such elevated mood that everyone was charmed.

And in my artistic life too, the day is of much importance. My wife recognized this also and rejoiced more in the success of my Symphony than in her own success. Forward then, with God's guidance on this path."

A note of romantic interest was struck with the coming of a gifted young composer, Johannes Brahms, into the Schumann home as a student. He was accepted immediately as a member of the family and became the idolized "Uncle Brahms" of the children. The pathos of his hopeless adoration for Clara was to last throughout his life. To this love he gave expression in his enchanting Lullaby, which was composed as he watched by the bedside of little Judy who lay ill with measles—Judy who was his favorite among the children because her eyes were blue like her mother's.

The Gemini rhythms set their impress upon all of Schumann's music. This is noted in the light, almost elfin quality of so many of his compositions; also in the quick succession of changing harmonies and his distinctive originality. This airy and graceful quality is especially exemplified in his *Papillons* (butterflies); regarding it he stated: "The air is so sweet and heavenly that I can wish for nothing but a carriage made of roses for an army of butterflies to draw home with gold and silver threads."

As his physical life neared its close, his sensitivity increased. He often held converse wtih beings of inner realms and wrote themes which, he said, were dictated to him by Angels. To the uncomprehending he was surely mad, as are all whose consciousness extends beyond common bounds. About his contacts with supersensible reality, he once declared that the "lovely light" bewitched him and enkindled in him such a sense of security that the storms of life no longer frightened him.

Upon Clara's last visit to him in the hospital, he roused himself and, stumbling to the piano, whispered brokenly, "I want to play something I have written for you." As the soft, tender cadences of *Traumerei* filled the little room his lifeless body fell across the keyboard. His spirit had waited only for the coming of his beloved Clara.

Schumann's color-tone was rose-pink, the love color, and his music is effective in counteracting depression and melancholia.

Could it have been for this reason that Clara Wieck Schumann devoted the remainder of her life to keeping alive the memory of her husband through her brilliant concertizing of his compositions? *Traumerei* was ever on her programs, and it was the final number of her last concert in the Royal Opera in Dresden. Though she still commanded the admiring plaudits of her audiences, Clara Schumann then retired, being well advanced in years. The day may come when we shall be wise enough to realize that a familiar piece of music that has been well beloved, and often enjoyed together by those whose spirits are in close accord, is a bridge of communion between the realms of the living and the so-called dead. Doubtless Clara Schumann held this secret close to her heart, and no doubt knew whereof she spoke when she said, "It is in the music of Robert Schumann that the angels sing."

# Chapter IV

## CANCER—Cherubim

THE HIERARCHY of Cancer is known as the Cherubim, whose mission has ever been to guard this planet's holy places. The Cherubim stand before the gates of Eden, that perfect etheric garden lost to man because of his unworthiness. A regenerated race will eventually re-enter the realm beautiful, so the Cherubim keep watch until that glad day. They also guard the Holy of Holies of the etheric Tabernacle, prototype of the Atlantean Mystery Temple. The Holy of Holies symbolizes the ultimate attainment of humanity as a whole. To this end the Cherubim teach man how to use rather than abuse what should be his most treasured possessions, the holy waters and the sacred seed of life.

The Cherubim's contact with the earth is through the exalted spiritual realm known as the World of Virgin Spirits. Therefore, their work has been passed down to the opposite sign Capricorn, the archangelic Hierarchy. The Lord Christ, highest of the Archangels, came to this plane bearing the message of purity and chastity. He taught that only the pure in heart should see God, and that we must be born of water and of fire (transmutation) before we can enter the kingdom of heaven.

The musical keynote of Cancer is G sharp major. The music most compatible to Cancer natives deifies the feminine or mother principle—music such as the lovely old Irish ballade *Mother McCree,* lullabies and tender cradle songs. Brahms' exquisite *Lullaby* is recommended for lifting their consciousness to higher realms; also Gustav Mahler's supreme work, *The Resurrection Symphony*. At the Christmas Season Cancer, the exalted mother sign, adorns midheaven and suffuses the atmosphere of earth with the fragrance of tenderness, love, compassion and sacrifice, qualities characteristic of true motherhood.

In this sign there is a gleaming nebula composed of stars and called Praesepe, meaning *the manger*. On either side of it are minute star clusters called Ascelli, the *little asses*, the gentle beasts that provide a colorful background in the manger legend which relates how one of the baby asses guarded the sacred crib and became the faithful companion of the infant Jesus.

Near to Cancer are the brilliant blue-white stars that form the constellation Auriga. The brightest of these is Capella, sometimes called the *shepherd star*. It is a star of the first magnitude and its name really means *she-goat*. Surrounding it like many children are a number of small stars in the form of a triangle; these are very appropriately referred to as "the kids." The oriental name for Capella translates into "messenger of light."

At the midnight hour of Holy Night Virgo is rising on the eastern horizon. This constellation is depicted as a maiden bearing two sheaves of golden wheat, a perfect symbol of the conception. Cancer is the human mother as represented by the madonna and child; Virgo is the enthroned, glorified Madonna typifying the Initiate-Mother. The sextile between these two signs is an index of the close cooperative bond between the two states of being.

In the celestial hand of the constellation of the Virgin is Spica, another magnificent star of the first magnitude referred to as "the diamond of the Virgin." In the Golden Age of Greece Temples were dedicated to this star in recognition of the nature and quality of its spiritual radiation. For it must be remembered that the stars we behold are the physical vehicles of indwelling spiritual Beings, a fact recognized by the wise men of all ages.

High in the heavens and moving toward the western horizon is the dominant figure of mighty Orion, a constellation containing a mysterious dark nebula which the Ancient Wisdom declares to be a doorway to other universes probably more vast than ours. In this constellation are three brilliant stars which, in the symbology we are following, are designated as the *Three Wise Men* who are successful in their search for the newborn Christ Child. In this connection it is interesting to note the color radiations of these three stars. Gigantic Betelgeuse, a star of the first magnitude that is 215,000,000 miles in diameter, is a brilliant red; Bellatrix is green-yellow while Rigel is blue-white.

Relating this to a particular legend about the Wise Men, brings out an interesting correspondence. This legend tells us that one of the Three Wise Men was a youth, the second was of middle age, the third was very old. Now red is the color belonging to young souls. It is identified with Martian exuberance and activity, with the aggressive, self-assertive side of man's nature. The gift of the young Wise Man was myrrh—which means *bitterness,* the bitterness of sorrow resulting from unwise, inexperienced living, yet the means whereby youth awakens to a recognition of the soul's higher values. Yellow correlates with the wisdom that comes with years. The gift of the second Wise Man was frankincense, typifying the fragrance of wisdom that comes with soul growth. Blue represents spirit. It belongs to the Father principle, the Ancient of Days. So the most aged of the three, in conformity with the color assigned to him, bore to the Christ Child the gift of gold, symbol of pure spirit and the signature of a mature or perfected soul.

Two glorious blue-white stars serve as celestial torch bearers in the processional of Virgo, the Blessed Lady of the skies. They are Sirius and Procyon. The latter leads, the former follows. Of the fixed stars, Sirius is the nearest to earth; even so, its distance is eight and a half light years away. It has been said that if all the diamonds of earth were melted into one, the brilliance of Sirius in a December sky would make that one appear pale by comparison. According to the Ancient Wisdom, the Hierarchy of that star will become the guardian and teacher of our planet when, at some future time, humanity has attained to a development where it can establish direct conscious contact with the Hierarchies that supervise our evolution.

## CANCER—*Cherubim*

The climax of the Holy Season comes with the birth of the new Sun in Capricorn on the night of the Winter Solstice. Of all the signs in the Zodiac, Capricorn, the sign on the topmost point of the natural chart, conceals the deepest mysteries and is, therefore, appropriately the sign under which Masters of all ages have chosen to take embodiment. It provides the most favorable vibratory conditions for saviours of the race to fulfill their earthly missions.

Constellations, like individual stars, ray forth a color-tone of their own. Cancer and Capricorn are blue-white; Virgo, a golden yellow. The collective keynote of all the stars in a constellation and, in turn, of all the constellations, compose the celestial Music of the Spheres. Earthly celebrations of the Nativity, in which color and music play so prominent a part, are a faint reflection of what is taking place in the heavens above.

When we are observant of these similitudes between events terrestrial and events celestial, we can better appreciate the song of the Psalmist as he gave expression to his joy in the cosmic grandeur that surrounded him. In his exaltation he sang: "The heavens declare the glory of God: and the firmament sheweth his handywork" (the celesial patterns we have noted). "Day unto day uttereth speech" (the songs of the stars), "and night unto night sheweth his knowledge" (the workings of spiritual law). "Their line is gone out through all the earth" (the powerful, far-reaching influence of the stars). "In them hath he set a tabernacle for the sun" (the homage that the heavens pay to the Blessed Lord Christ, the radiant Archangel of the Sun). Around this sublime Being and His sacrifice for earth and humanity are centered the beautiful Christ-mass mysteries — mysteries we find duplicated in the glories of both heaven and earth.

### GUSTAV MAHLER — 1860-1911

Cancer is a deeply mystical sign, one of intense soul ecstasy. Its natives are extremely sensitive and have a tendency toward dreamy introspection. Such a mystical dreamer was the highly gifted, but largely misunderstood and greatly underrated, Cancerian Gustav Mahler. The signature of the elusive Cancer which pervades his music is a necessary background for true appreciation of his works.

Some form of spiritual fuel was so essential to the creative fires of this budding young genius that from his early youth he was prone to clothe the most trivial and commonplace affairs in enigmatic raiment. His earliest efforts at composition centered in fairy-like themes or ephemeral abstractions. As his musical genius developed and expanded, "Art became his religion, the conductor's stand an altar and the score a ritual."

Mahler's temperament was such that he naturally became one of the most ardent pro-Wagnerites of his day. Doubtless the inspiration for his early career came about during his attendance at a Beyreuth production of *Parsifal* in the summer of 1883. He refers to it thus: "As I emerged from the Festspielhaus too moved to utter a word I knew that the loftiest and most agonizing of revelations had just come to me and that it would remain with me throughout my life." It was under this inspiration that he composed his beautiful *Resurrection Symphony*.

Typically Cancer, Mahler was a devout nature worshiper. His sensitive soul was torn with sorrow when he cried, "O my beloved Earth, O when will you take the abandoned one into your lap! See mankind has driven him forth and he flees from its cold, heartless bosom to you, to you! Receive the lonely, restless one, O eternal Mother." He found both comfort and courage in the "holy place of nature," and also the devotional impulse he has woven into his symphonies. We find him incorporating songs of the flowers and voices of the winds into his music. He wrote: "I climb the hills caressed by the breath of God. I go to the meadows where the tinkling of the herd-bells lulls me to dreaming."

Of the many Mahler symphonies, special mention must be given to the colossal *Eighth* which, in its profound implications and magnificence of concept, takes its place along with

Beethoven's *Ninth*. Says the composer regarding this symphony: "Imagine that the whole Universe begins to sound in tone. The result is not merely human voices singing but a vision of planets and suns coursing about." This stupendous work—"the Symphony of a thousand" as it is often called by reason of the augmented orchestra and the large chorus required for its presentation—was given its dual American premiere by Leopold Stokowski in New York and in Philadelphia in 1916. During the 1948 season of *Symphonies under the Stars* in Hollywood Bowl it was given its first West Coast hearing under the inspired direction of Eugene Ormandy.

The color note of Cancer is a shimmering leaf-green shot through with silver. Mahler's color note bears this green-silver sheen into which is interblended the soft blue of devotion. This blue tone is especially pronounced in the music of the *Eighth Symphony*.

The music of this New Age composer, who catches the rhythms of the incoming Aquarian Age, may be used to develop psychic ability and etheric vision, and to awaken latent spiritual centers. It is also effective in the cultivation of a sense of beauty, an attribute so greatly neglected in this mechanized era. Without it the gracious, harmonious order of the New Day can never be realized. The highest significance of Mahler's genius may be said to consist in its power to lead its hearers into a divine "adventure of the soul" where the seen and the unseen are one and where this life and the after-life merge into a unity.

*Chapter V*

## LEO—The Lords of Flame

IN THE constellation Leo, the Lion, are a number of brilliant stars. Six of these outline the lion's head, others are in each of the four paws. Across one of the forepaws shines Regulus, a star of the first magnitude and one of the brightest in the heavens, whose red-gold light gleams across the sky with all the brilliance of a million candles. In the lion's tail is Denebola, likewise a star of surpassing brilliance. The lion found depicted on ruins throughout Chaldea, Babylon and Persia attests to the importance given to this constellation by ancient people. Its importance goes back, no doubt, to the period when the Summer Solstice occurred in the sign Leo.

The fiery script of the stars contains not only the story of human evolution, but also outlines the Path of Initiation as taught in Mystery Temples of old. In the intimate connection between the sign Leo and the next adjoining sign Virgo, symbolized by a feminine figure, is to be found the origin of the Egyptian Sphinx – part of a Mystery Temple – where the head of a woman is joined to the body of a lion.

All of the fire signs are transmutative in their power and action. One of the most sacred of early day hieroglyphics is a symbolic representation of the Sphinx. It depicts a young maiden standing beside a crouched lion and closing its mouth with her hands, symbolic of the ultimate attainment of the initiatory quest whereby the brute force or animalistic aspect of man's nature is subdued and transmuted through the power of spirit.

The Hierarchy of Leo, Lords of Flame, aided humanity in its early development by awakening the highest side of his threefold nature, and by radiating from their fiery center that which became the very essence of man's physical body. This Hierarchy has also progressed beyond our solar system, contacting it only from the high plane known as the World of Virgin Spirits. Its work of awakening in humanity the power of life has been transferred to its opposite and complementary sign, Aquarius.

The Lord Christ gave us the divine formula for applying the power of love when He said, "Thou shalt love the Lord thy God with all thy heart (and) thy neighbor as thyself." In this divided and disturbed world there is but little concept or understanding of loving one's neighbor as one's self, but the Hierarchy of Aquarius will aid the human race in its development. In the Aquarian Age the glorious ideal of the Fatherhood of God and the brotherhood of man will become a reality in the hearts and lives of men.

The musical keynote of Leo is A sharp major. Relaxation and renewal for Leo natives will be found in the music of Claude Debussy, music that is both stimulating and inspiring. Particularly suitable as an accompaniment to prayer and meditation because of its mystical quality is the score of *Pelleas and Melisande;* also, the *Afternoon of a Faun,* wherein the ideal and the actual forces of the inner and outer world meet and unite. As previously observed, the fire signs are all transmutative in nature. For Leo natives who are working with the processes of transmutation we would suggest "power music" whereby purely human forces are sublimated into spiritual forces. Such music is provided by Beethoven's symphonies.

## ACHILLE CLAUDE DEBUSSY — 1862-1918

It is natural that a Leo should be attracted by things leonine. In the case of Debussy this fact was conspicuous in his great love for cats, household pets that come under the rulership of Leo. Debussy's strongly marked feline likes and characteristics occasioned no little comment among his intimates. Andre Saures, in his *Literary Portrait of the Composer,* observed that "just as a cat rubs itself against the hand which strokes it, so Debussy caresses his soul with the pleasure which he invokes."

In his home Debussy surrounded himself with cats, Angoras being his favorite breed. His passion for the felines is well illustrated by the following incident. It was a day when his cupboard was bare so he reluctantly disposed of one of his early piano pieces to buy food. Did he purchase at the market the edibles his physical hunger demanded? Not so! Instead he bought a porcelain cat to adorn his apartment. He carried his cat-fancying to the point that his favorite Parisian rendezvous was the celebrated Chat Noir, its name being in homage to the huge crouched feline figure done in forged iron which served as a sign. Here Debussy consorted with contemporary artists of his day.

In common with the pets he loved so much, Debussy loved solitude. He was also of an artistic and amorous nature. Despite his feline movements – slow, deliberate and graceful – he was deeply passionate when aroused. His creative genius was distinctly New Age. Debussy was aptly described in his own country by the expressive phrase "Tres exceptionnel, tres curieux, tres solitaire."

Debussy's music was a bridge between the music of a passing age and that of an incoming age. As a New Age composer, it was his constant aim to bring about what he termed "freedom of music." He declared, "I try always to free music from the barren traditions which stifle it. I am for liberty. Music by its very nature is free. Every sound you hear around you can be reproduced. Everything that the keen ear perceives in the rhythms of the surrounding world can be represented musically." Thus it is that in Debussy we are in the presence of one of nature's high priests of music. To him the primary purpose was not to reproduce the musical rhythms of nature, but to interpret the relationship existing between nature and man. His establishment of this accord was due in part to the nature spirits. Hence, his music can best be described as an interpretation of nature and of nature's messengers.

This inspired interpreter had a gift for depicting festivals of the future as they would be when man came into a more harmonious relationship with nature, on which subject Debussy had this to say: "I can imagine music especially designed for the open air, all on big lines with daring instrumental and vocal effects which would have full play in the open and soar joyously to the tree tops. Certain harmonic progressions which sound abnormal within the four walls of a concert hall would find their true value in the open air . . . Thus art might find regeneration and learn the beautiful lesson of freedom from the efflorescence of the trees . . . So the very air, movement of leaves, the perfume of flowers would work together in mysterious union with music which would bring all the elements into such natural harmony that it would seem to form a part of each. In this way it could be proved that music and poetry, alone of the arts, dwell in space. It is my belief that this idea will be the dream of future generations."

The strange harmonies characteristic of Debussy's music marked him from the beginning of his creative work as a revolutionary in the harmonic sense. They sound many of the nature spirit rhythms that are inaudible to the average person's hearing, but were caught by this devotee and reproduced through the ecstasy of his adoration.

Debussy was also a poet and a painter, though what he had to express through these arts found more adequate expression in his musical scores. He was a poet of night and of dawn, of moonlight and of velvet shadows, of mists and of perfume, and was, at the same time, a painter of dryads and fauns, of arabesques and fantasies so delicate and ethereal that their forms quiver in soft outlines of harmony only to dissolve quickly before our wondering and enchanted vision.

Never a formal religionist, nature was Debussy's god and his adoration of her manifestations was his religion. Although none of his hundred or more compositions can be termed sacred music in the orthodox sense, yet his intimate attunement with nature forces enabled him to make audible the voices of Angels and fairies, dryads and nymphs—a truly spiritual contribution to our time.

It is significant that in the last years of his waning health, Debussy turned with increasing interest to the works of two superb poets of the invisible, Shakespeare and Edgar Allen Poe. He said that Poe "possessed the most original fantasy among the literature of all lands" and that he sounded "a note absolutely new and different." Debussy set out to create operas based on Poe's tales. Unfortunately, these were never finished although the Metropolitan Opera Association of New York had secured the rights to produce them.

From twenty-eight to thirty-eight was the golden decade of this artist's life. During that period he produced *The Afternoon of a Faun,* the Nocturnes and many of his best piano pieces, together with *Pelleas and Melisande.* The last is Debussy's only completed opera. In the Wagnerian manner, this French artist employed motifs descriptive of each character, which are usually introduced immediately in advance of the character's appearance. They are decidedly the most outstanding feature of Debussy's music. Laurence Gilman, the late brilliant music-analyst, defines them as "sound-wraiths, misty and evanescent rather than clearly defined, harmonic half-lights and melodic shreds, more suggestive and evocative than descriptive and definitive."

Debussy passed from earthly existence March 25, 1918, while all France was shrouded in sorrow for the wounded and dead. Music of the latter's funeral procession was heavy cannonading that was going on both near at hand and afar off. Later, with the signing of peace, a magnificent monument was erected in honor of "Claude Debussy, musician Francais" which is as ultra modern as are his compositions. It was designed as a spiritual interpretation of his work, and contains allegorical figures of the various characters described in his music. These include Pelleas and Melisande, the faun, nymphs, satyrs, fairies, the sea, the cathedral, the clouds, and a figure of the musician himself seated at a piano and surrounded by famous contemporaries. This tapestry in stone stands against a background of trees and flowers. It is reflected in the water of a pool at its foot, a fitting symbol of the reflection of the inner world in the music of one who declared that it was "his sole purpose to write down his musical dreams and to sing his interior visions in a spirit of utter self-detachment."

Debussy's color note was jade green. It is related that from early childhood the composer was literally enchanted with the color green. It was so necessary to his comfort and well-being that he wore something green or had the color near enough so he could feast his eyes upon it. This affinity for green was both natural and inevitable since his avowed purpose was to create music that makes man more cognizant of nature's finer forces. The green that is nature's basic color may be seen extending into etheric realms where it assumes the clearest, most exquisite tones of soft jade. This was the color-tone through which Debussy received his highest inspiration.

# Chapter VI

## VIRGO—The Lords of Wisdom

Virgo is the only constellation represented by a feminine figure: a beautiful maiden outlined in stars, her right hand raised as though blessing the world. In her left hand she holds a sheaf of wheat adorned by one of the Zodiac's most magnificent lights—Spica, another star of the first magnitude.

From earliest times man has pictured divine law as manifest throughout nature as feminine in form. Many temples erected by early civilizations were dedicated to the worship of the Virgin Goddess and her radiant star, and all great world religions found their prototype in Virgo. She is the Ishtar of Babylon, the Isis of Egypt, the Persephone of Greece, the Ceres of Rome. To her were ascribed the seasonal changes, the cold darkness of winter and the warm brightness of summer.

When the Egyptian Isis went in search of the body of Osiris, the earth put on somber robes of mourning; when she returned she brought with her the shimmering garb of gladness. In Greece Persephone, the beautiful daughter of Demeter (Roman Ceres), was gathering flowers in the forest when she was carired away by Pluto, God of the Underworld. The earth wept as the mother searched for her daughter. Flowers and fruits languished and harvest fields were bare. Then Jupiter decreed that Persephone must be restored to her mother six months of the year; those were the months when beauty and abundance reigned on earth.

The Babylonian Goddess Ishtar journeyed through the seven gates leading to the Underworld in search of her dead husband. At each of these gates she was required to surrender some of her possessions. At the entrance to the seventh gate she stood completely nude. She had nothing more to give. This is a veiled story of the seven Lesser Mysteries upon which ancient religions were founded. The mystic key is the same to both ancient and modern Temple teachings: before one can receive all he must be willing to renounce all. Service and sacrifice are the keynotes of Initiation, of motherhood and of Virgo.

The Hierarchy of Virgo is comprised of the Lords of Wisdom, who contact this planet by means of the sphere known as the World of Divine Spirits, highest of the spiritual realms. At the beginning of human evolution the Hierarchy of Virgo awakened within developing man a spark of the Christ Consciousness, and radiated from themselves the germ of that essence which was to become his vital or etheric body. Their present work with mankind is to teach the true meaning and purpose of wisdom. Wisdom has been defined as "crystallized pain." It is the distilled essence of experience: of pain and pleasure, sorrow and joy, darkness and light. Under the tutelage of the Lords of Virgo, man is slowly but surely developing true soul-wisdom.

The musical keynote of Virgo is F natural. Virgo is an earth sign and its natives are compatible with all nature music. Relief from nervous tension, physical renewal and mental stimulation will be attained by the music of Sibelius and Grieg. As an accompaniment to periods of prayer and meditation, we recommend Beethoven's *Pastoral* and *Sixth Symphony*.

## GIACOMO MEYERBEER — 1791 - 1864

Giacomo Meyerbeer was born in Berlin September 5, 1791. His father, a Hebrew, was one of Prussia's richest citizens, and his three brothers grew up to be men of distinction. Giacomo's fame eclipsed them all, for he won a place of greatest importance in the history of nineteenth century musical art. From his childhood he showed evidence of remarkable talent, and at the age of nine gave his first public concert in Berlin at which he made a lasting impression on all who heard him.

Proud of his young son's genius, his father spared neither time nor money in procuring for him every possible musical advantage. Outstanding in both performance and composition, the youth was finally brought to the attention of the celebrated Abbe Vogler, whose School of Music was, perhaps, the most famous of his day, and he himself was among the foremost theoreticians of the time. Meyerbeer spent a number of years as a member of the Abbe's school, where he formed the beautiful and lasting friendship with Carl von Weber which grew more and more intimate until the latter passed.

The theory and discipline of the Vogler school were representative of the concept that music was a sacred art and should be pursued in a serious and reverent attitude. The house of Abbe Vogler was patriarchal, the students devoting themselves entirely to spiritual contemplation, serious study and practice. Each morning the maestro gave his pupils an oral lesson in counterpoint, after which they were assigned some musical subject—often something sacred such as a psalm, kyrie, ode or dramatic scene. Taking it as a basis, they were required to create a composition of their own. In the evening the pupils were assembled to hear the teacher perform, dissect and criticize each composition in turn.

This procedure was perfect training for the Virgo mind and temperment of Giacomo Meyerbeer. The thoroughness of his Virgo nature made him seek exacting analysis and constructive criticism as a means of helping him to greater achievement. His goal was perfection. Also the spiritual atmosphere of the house was most congenial to this student as the innate purity of the Virgo native is in harmony with all that pertains to the higher life.

On Sundays the entire student body went to the cathedral where there were two organs. The Abbe took his place at one while each of the pupils played the other in turn. This became a sort of academic tournament, the highest score being made by that pupil who best developed the theme improvised by the maestro.

During his school days Meyerbeer composed a number of sacred odes and oratorios which he held ever after as being too sacred to be made public. Then it was that his soul experienced the deep spiritual realization that made such a marked impress upon his later work—*The Hugenots* and *Le Prophete,* for example, compositions which earned him the reputation of being the finest composer of his time.

Meyerbeer was to attain to his greatest heights in Paris. Neither Germany nor Italy fed the divine spark of genius within him sufficiently for it to come into its most perfect flowering. This honor was reserved for France, where destiny guided him and brought him into his own. It was in France that he found the inspiration for his four great operas: *The Hugenots, Le Prophete, Robert Le Diable* and *L'Africaine.* The last did not have its premiere until a year after the composer's death, which occurred in Paris May 2nd, 1864.

Meyerbeer was doubtless the greatest dramatic musician prior to Richard Wagner. The following musically biographical paragraph about him might easily appear in an astrological textbook delineating the characteristics of Virgo: "He neglected no detail, no effect, no method that enabled him to augment his resources, to complete his thought, in a word to attain perfection. Nothing dismayed him, he spared no pains to realize his ideal, to obtain the result at which he aimed, and he never felt that he had done a thing so well that it could not be improved. Thus his works have the solidity of marble and the strength of iron. And if a blemish be sometimes discovered in them, it is like the spots on the sun, which do not interfere with its dazzling light."

Meyerbeer's color note was pale, soft yellow and his music may be used for intensifying spiritual perception.

*Chapter VII*

## LIBRA—The Lords of Individuality

FAR BACK in man's most remote history there were only ten signs of the Zodiac. *Ten* was the number of the ancients and *ten* was the number of the Old Testament Dispensation. Preparations for the coming of the Lord Christ were made aeons before His appearance on earth. Forces of the number ten were then raised to the powers of number twelve, for *twelve* is the number of the New Testament Dispensation.

When there were only ten zodiacal signs Virgo and Scorpio were united. Later, these two signs were separated and Libra, the Scales or Balance, was placed between them. It is not known by whom this alteration was effected, although it has been ascribed to the Egyptians because the scales, signifying balance, were a most important factor in their religion. According to the Egyptian scriptures, *The Book of the Dead,* the heart of anyone newly deceased was weighed in the presence of the God Osiris. A feather was put on one side of the scales and the heart on the other. If the feather was lighter than the heart, its owner had to pass into the darkness of the Underworld. If the heart was lighter than the feather, his soul ascended into the realms of bliss.

Libra is also the sign of the Autumn Equinox when, for an interval of four days and four nights, perfect equilibrium exists between the hours of light and of darkness. As one poet expresses it,

> *Then Day and Night in Libra's Scales*
> *are weighed Equal a while.*

It has been previously stated that the starry script outlines not only the course of human evolution, but also the Path of

Initiation. Libra is the Trial Gate between Virgo, the way of spirit, and Scorpio, the way of the senses. At the time of his dedication, every aspirant must stand before this Trial Gate and make his choice. The decision is not made once and for all time; it must be made again and again — for as the Path becomes steeper and narrower, the temptations thereon become more subtle. For example, a disciple of many years duration no longer needs testings relative to his physical body, such as foregoing alcohol, meat and tobacco. They are already obnoxious to him. His testings will be related to a willingness to renounce long cherished plans and personal desires that he may work for the good of others. *Light on the Path* admonishes aspirants to kill out personal ambition, yet to continue working as do those who are ambitious. Time after time, life after life, a disciple must stand before the Trial Gate of Libra until the Great White Work is consummated.

The Shining Ones of the Hierarchy of Libra are known as the Lords of Individuality. They contact the earth by means of the World of Life Spirit, also known as the realm of Christed Consciousness. At the outset of human evolution this Hierarchy radiated from itself the divine seed germ of man's emotional body. Now it is working with pioneers of the human race to bring about a higher individualization of its egos. The Lords of Individuality are teaching those who will accept their instruction how each individual ego may become one with the whole.

The musical keynote of Libra is D major. It is a sign of harmony, love and beauty, so the Libran native is closely attuned to music wherein these qualities predominate. For relaxation, renewal of the physical and mental bodies, inspiration, and awakening of one's spiritual faculties, the music of Libra's own son is recommended. We refer to Giuseppe Verdi, the celebrated musical genius.

The color pattern in which Verdi's music is centered is a soft, deep rose, often called old rose. This is the humanitarian love color.

## GIUSEPPE VERDI — 1813-1901

Giuseppe Verdi, master of lyric melody and of truly Libran heritage, was born October 10, 1813, in the small Italian village of Roncole, home of approximately two hundred impoverished peasants. Like most of the members of his community, he was born into a life of dire poverty. Italy was then made up of many restless and impotent little states under the yoke of foreign domination. Raised amid community inharmony, political and social, and extreme financial stringency in his home, Verdi's heart was touched by the struggle and aspirations of humanity at large, and his selfless sympathy found release in lyric music. His compositions gave expression to the Italian people's dream of freedom, their rebellion against bondage, and their intense love of the beautiful.

Verdi made a masterly musical transcription of the sheer ecstasy that an Italian experiences as he does homage before the shrine of beauty. His was the musical voice of his country, pleading her cause before all the people of earth; and his fellow countrymen came to recognize this fact during Verdi's lifetime.

Although he had requested that his funeral be carried out with the utmost lack of ostentation, the entire Italian populace observed his passing with obsequies glorifying the one who had contributed so greatly to the cultural riches of the nation. On the day of the funeral the nation rose *en massé* at dawn to pay honor while his glorious music was broadcast to his native land and to the world at large. The famous conductor, Arturo Toscanini, led a chorus of nine hundred voices; and spontaneously an audience of no less than three thousand joined in the singing. Among that throng was golden-voiced Enrico Caruso. The selections were taken from *Nabuco,* one of Verdi's earliest and best loved operas.

Verdi's entrance upon the physical plane was hailed by strolling players who came to sing their greeting under the windows where he lay. His return to higher realms was to the accompaniment of his own music as the voices of the Italian people were lifted in songs of thanksgiving, blessing Verdi for the joy and beauty he had brought into their lives. It was fitting indeed that the spirit of this great lyricist should be enfolded in waves of ineffable harmony both at the beginning of his life and upon its triumphant conclusion.

Giuseppe's Guardian Angels were verily of the musical Ray, and numerous are the recorded instances of their divine protection. When he was but an infant in arms, the little village of his nativity was invaded by a band of boisterous, carousing Cossacks. Women and children fled to the church for sanctuary. Giuseppe's mother hid him and herself far up in the bell tower, where they remained safe until the last of the soldiers rode away.

The lad's genius was so marked and his progress so rapid that while he was only ten years old he was contributing to the family income by playing an organ in a nearby village. One dark night he was returning home on foot when he fell into a deep ditch swollen by recent rains. The boy called until his strength failed him, then slipped into unconsciousness. He awakened to hear a neighbor saying, "It's the Verdi boy! The angels must be watching over you Son. I just chanced to be passing. No paradise for you yet; you're meant to stay on this earth."

Another instance occurred as he was attending vespers. Arriving late, he took a seat among the congregation instead of his usual place in the choir. A violent thunder storm came up during the service and lightening struck the church, killing three persons in the choir loft and two priests at the altar, yet the congregation was unharmed.

Space does not permit a detailed account of the struggles and disappointments that beset this musical genius. It has been said "his courage was limitless and his determination granite." True to the pendulum swing of Libra, Verdi knew the extremes of poverty in his youth and the good fortune that comes later with fame and adulation. After the La Scala performance of one of his most popular operas, the city of Milan was *en fete* all through the night. Verdi's hotel was lavishly decorated. The horses were removed from his carriage so he and his beloved wife Pappinna could be carried in the arms of a shouting multitude all the way from the opera house to the hotel.

Verdi's popularity reached its climax with the premiere of *Aida,* the opera written to commemorate the opening of both Cairo's new opera house and the Suez Canal. The spectacular brilliance of the opera itself (which still remains by acclaimation the world's favorite) was matched by the magnificent display of audience notables from all over the world, gathered to honor the Italian maestro's greatest work. His triumph was repeated with the first performance of *Aida* at La Scala on February 8, 1872. Never had the flame of popularity blazed more brilliantly for Verdi than on that night. A few admiring peasants had created the initial rung on his ladder of success. At fifty-eight his audience was international, their plaudits, sounding 'round the world, carried him to the topmost rung of that ladder.

The genius of Verdi was so prolific that comparatively early in life he had produced seventeen operas. In his youth he was called affectionately "maestrino," meaning *little master*. But not until *Rigoletto* did his music take on the note of immortality. The superb aria *La Donna e Mobile* won instant acclaim, and continues to this day to be in great favor. *Don Carlos, Macbeth, Il Trovatore, La Traviata, Otello* and *Falstaff* are all jewels of increasing lustre in the crown of fame so firmly placed upon the brow of Italy's supremely gifted musical son.

Verdi's music is in almost complete attunement with the Italian race spirit. It is, as it were, the embodiment of national idealism and inspiration. In his works Italy is face to face with its very own soul, and is rejoicing over the beauties it discovers therein through the magic of Giuseppe's musical power to penetrate to inner realities that are ever pure and perfect.

*Chapter VIII*

## SCORPIO—The Lords of Form

A scorpion is a malefic animal that prefers night to day, darkness to light. It seems to bear slight relationship to its namesake, the constellation of Scorpio wherein is gathered such a galaxy of glittering stars as to make its brilliance unsurpassed in the heavens. In the constellation the creature's head is outlined in stars, they adorn its claws and its curving tail in a shimmer of light. Centered in the very heart of the Scorpion is the famous red star Antares. A star of the first magnitude, its ruddy glow out-rivals that of the planet Mars. Despite the brilliance and beauty of this constellation, it has often been associated with darkness and death. The ancient lore of many lands attributes the fall of man to the powers of Scorpio.

As the plan of human evolution and the Path of Initiation are outlined in the stars, so also is the eternal struggle between good and evil. On the opposite side of the heavens from Scorpio is one of the sky's most dazzling spectacles, the constellation of Orion. The celestial hunter stands upright, his head surrounded by a stellar halo. His belt is comprised of three famous lights and others gleam from his shoulders. One of them is Betelgeuse, also of the first magnitude, whose lustrious red light illumines the whole area round about. Adorning one side of his body is Rigel (first magnitude) whose blue-white light gleams like a benediction.

The merest amateur among astronomers is familiar with the dark nebula located within this constellation. It is said, esoterically, that in some future day stellar explorers will be able to penetrate this mysterious nebula and discover that it is a doorway opening upon far more wondrous universes than the mind of man can now conceive.

Orion is a veritable god of beauty and light. He rises as the Scorpion sets, and disappears from view as the Scorpion ascends, thus continuing the symbolic struggle between darkness and light. Orion is identified with Marduke, Sun God of the Babylonians; Ra, Sun God of the Egyptians; Phaeton, Sun God of the Greeks. It was Phaeton who, in his chariot drawn by fiery steeds, attempted to visit all the constellations. He passed safely through them until he reached Scorpio, where one of the horses felt the sting of the Scorpion and plunged downward. Phaeton and his chariot fell to their destruction on the earth below. This was a Greek legend relative to the Fall of man, and the people said this disaster occurred as the Sun was transiting the sign Scorpio.

The Lords of Form make up the Hierarchy of Scorpio. They contact the earth through that sphere known as the World of Abstract Thought. In early stages of human evolution the Hierarchy of Scorpio taught humanity how to build form. In order for man to function on the physical plane and learn earth's lessons it was necessary that he should have a body composed of physical substance. This was the body that the Lords of Form taught man how to fashion. They still continue to teach humanity how to build bodies, but of ever increasing refinement and sensitivity. So they give instruction in the science of transmutation, the most advanced work of a disciple.

The lower side of Scorpio is represented by the scorpion having the sting of death. The higher side of this sign is represented by an eagle, the majestic bird whose delight is flying straight into the face of the Sun. Scorpio is a sign possessing tremendous power, its keywords being *transmutation* and *sublimation*. In the light of this knowledge ancient alchemists recognized that the most propitious time for transmuting base metal into gold was when the Sun was transiting Scorpio.

The musical keynote of Scorpio is E major. Franz Liszt, a highly gifted artist, was a native of Scorpio. Sometimes he indulged in physical excesses, but he never lost sight of his high idealism. Liszt's color pattern was a clear, deep steel blue shot through with brilliant sparks of gold and silver.

For physical refreshment and mental stimulation Liszt's beautiful Hungarian dances are recommended. For an advanced disciple working with the forces of transmutation, we suggest his Oratorios *St. Elizabeth* and *Christos;* also any of his Masses. Richard Strauss' *Death and Transfiguration* might be added to this list.

## Franz Liszt — 1811-1886

Franz Liszt, a Scorpion native, can be more intelligently comprehended through an understanding of this most deeply mystical and enigmatic of the zodiacal signs. In his art and his life he expressed the power, the passion, the inspiration and the sublimity that characterize this sign.

Scorpio possesses the unfathomed depth and power of the sea. In conformity with its broad expanse, the Scorpio native chafes at restraint — a marked characteristic exhibited by Liszt in his personal life and in his music. His features, the lift of his head and shoulders, together with the untrammeled heights to which his genius soared, won for him the aptly descriptive title of "the dauntless eagle." The poet Saphir wrote of him: "Liszt knows no rules, no forms, no style. He creates his own. With him the bizarre becomes genial, the strange seems to become necessary." Scorpio is a powerful creative sign. It is the magnetic field wherein the forces of generation are operative. On its lower level these forces manifest as de-generation; on its higher level, as re-generation — as the two pictorial symbols for the sign indicate.

From his youth Liszt, true to the intensity of his Scorpio nature, responded to its higher influence. He was an ecstatic mystic, ardently yearning to renounce worldy aspirations and to give himself entirely to the service of God. At the age of nineteen the boy-artist, writing with the wisdom of a sage, observed that "the true artist must possess the faculty of dying to himself before he can give himself completely to others." The fire of his developing genius was fanned into white heat by long hours of meditation centered in Thomas à Kempis' *Imitation of Christ,* and by certain ascetic exercises he had evolved for himself. Had it not been for his father's firm interference at this time, young Franz would have thrown himself into the arms of the church. Toward the end of his life he did completely renounce the world and retreat into the seclusion of a monastery, where his art reached its highest perfection.

One born under Scorpio seems destined to soar more effortlessly toward the goal of his aspiration than those coming under other signs. Almost from his initial appearance as a child-artist, Liszt was a master of his chosen art. His triumphant performance at La Scala when at the flood-tide of his genius is described thus: "That which is properly the spirit, the very breath of genius, can only be experienced, but never described. Imagine a thin figure with narrow shoulders, his long hair falling over his face and down his neck, an extraordinarily spiritual face, pale, most interesting, an eye that reflects every thought, glittering in conversation and full of good will . . . When he sits down at the piano, he passes his hand through his hair, then his glance grows fixed, his breast calm, only his head and the expression of his face show the emotions he is experiencing. It is impossible to give any description of his playing, one must have heard him." So unusual were the qualities of this musician that he was sometimes referred to by his devotees as having "the face of a man-angel" and as possessing "a miraculous life."

After hearing him, Clara Schumann said, "Liszt can be compared to no other virtuoso. He is the only one of his kind. He arouses both fright and astonishment, though he is a very lovable artist." Another of her comments brings out the depth and power of his Scorpio nature: "His attitude at the piano," she wrote, "cannot be described. He is original, he grows sombre at the piano and his passions know no limit."

To like effect wrote another musical critic: "The audience look at one another, dumb with surprise, as after a sudden storm in a serene sky. And he, the Prometheus who with each note has forged a being, his head bent, smiles strangely before the crowds that applaud him madly."

In his personal life Liszt alternated between the heights where the eagle lifts undazzled eyes to the heart of the Sun and the low ground where crawls the scorpion to distill its poison. Liszt, unobserved, would often slip away from the cheering throng to spend the remaining hours of the night in church upon his knees. At other times he would take part in the sensual carousals so freely indulged in by those about him.

After visiting the great cathedral in Cologne, Liszt wrote to a friend: "I don't know why the sight of the cathedral always moves me strangely. Is it because music is an architecture of sound or because architecture is crystalized music? There certainly exists a close relationship between these two arts."

One of Liszt's finest qualities was his eager and unselfish desire to befriend unknown and struggling artists. Chopin, Schumann and Wagner found their way to fame paved by the kindly assistance of this man. He was responsible for the initial presentations of both *Tannhauser* and *Lohengrin.* He wrote to Wagner: "As a pious churchman underlines word by word the whole *Imitation of Jesus Christ,* I may easily come to the point of underlining note by note your Lohengrin."

The alternating impulses that spring from the higher and the lower natures of a Scorpio native were well described by Liszt in terms of his own experience: "I am still a part of this world, but my mind and heart dwell in regions little known to others." Despite his deflections, the glory of his art was always his soul's pole star. "True art is for the world's regeneration," he declared. And in the immortal glory of Liszt's music we find his true soul signature.

During the final decade of his life spent amid the quiet and peace of monastery gardens, so magnificent was the out-pouring of his genius in dedication to the church that he received the name of "Angelico of Music." It has been said that "He will never be surpassed; here he exhausts all the riches of form and metaphysics."

## The Cosmic Harp

Franz Liszt was born when the heavens were lighted by the spectacular grandeur of a great comet – an augury, perhaps, of a life whose radiance still illumines the horizon. "My sole ambition as a musician," said Liszt, "has been and will be to cast my javelin into the indefinite spaces of the future."

*Chapter IX*

## SAGITTARIUS—The Lords of Mind

SAGITTARIUS is the Archer; also the Centaur. The latter is formed of the upper part of a man's anatomy joined to the body of a horse. There are no stars of the first magnitude in Sagittarius but there are some rather brilliant ones. A bow and arrow are held in the Centaur's hands, the arrow pointed directly toward the heart of the Scorpion – Scorpio being the adjoining constellation – and three stars shine brightly in the bow. Five others form an aura about the Centaur's head. Then there is a sprinkling of stars scattered about the body of the horse to the end of its tail. Close beside the figure lies a beautiful crown encircled by five stars; this is the Crown Australis located near the equator.

Ancient history contains many fascinating allusions to strange creatures, half animal and half human. They are said to possess the wisdom and power of the gods, enabling them to perform miraculous feats among their associates. Perhaps the most famous of these was the Grecian Chiron who was the teacher of many Greek heroes such as Aesculapius, their patron saint of healing. Chiron taught this hero how to heal human ills and how to restore the dead to life. He also instructed his pupil in the power and magic of music as a panacea for all human ills.

The ancients, however, have left no information relative to the origin of these strange creatures. But when we turn to occult philosophy we find that the animal kingdom was guided and directed by Group Spirits, celestial Beings possessing miraculous power who ofttimes assumed forms that were part human and part animal when they were working with their animal charges. The naturally clairvoyant primitive people could watch these Beings at work, so their mythology and so-called fables were probably based on a retained memory.

The Hierarchy of Sagittarius is comprised of the Lords of Mind. They contact our planet by means of the World of Concrete Thought, which division of the spirit realms is designated as the Second Heaven. Early in human evolution the Lords of Mind radiated from themselves the shining essence containing the seed of the human mind. In other words, these great Beings bestowed upon man the priceless gift which lifts him above the animal kingdom and opens a way whereby he may become as a god. At the present time they are working to spiritualize the minds of the whole race — or, as it is expressed in metaphysical parlance, to teach man to Christ his mind.

This is a vitally important work because a highly trained but unillumined materialistic mind is the most sinister force in the world at the present time. St. Paul aptly termed it "the power of darkness." Such minds are being used by the Black Forces as their most responsive instruments for bringing about chaos, dissolution and the eventual destruction of the entire earthly realm. This is the crisis now confronting humanity. Never before in the history of the world has the work of the Lords of Mind been so greatly needed, and they pray for the cooperation of all God-loving individuals and groups.

F major is the musical keynote of Sagittarius, sign of the poet, the prophet, the mystic and the seer. A Sagittarian may have a center but he will never have a circumference. He may be centered in the finite but he will be reaching toward the infinite. Ludwig van Beetthoven was a true Sagittarian, and his music sounds the rhythms of other planets and of grander universes. It is indeed infinite music. For both physical and mental stimulation any or all of his beautiful piano concertos are recommended. For more profound spiritual work we suggest those most glorious of all musical compositions, Beethoven's nine symphonies.

## Ludwig van Beethoven — 1770-1828

Ludwig van Beethoven was, and still is, the high priest of the musical world, the supreme musical artist, the greatest master of them all. He was born December 16th, 1770. Sagittarius, his natal sign, is the zodiacal home of such as have lost sight of their personal selves that they may follow their higher selves unto the most distant star. The illumined Sagittarian is well described in the following quotation:

> *The prophetic soul of the wide world*
> *Dreaming on things to come.*

These lines are equally descriptive of the music of this Sagittarian who has been described variously as the great mystic tone poet; the metaphysician of the musical world; the musician who felt, thought and dreamed in tones.

Beethoven was without doubt an Illuminati of the Musical Ray, sent by invisible Hosts to perform a definite mission. He himself was well aware of that mission. The fact that it was not recognized by the world of his day was a source of deep regret to him. In fact, it was the chief tragedy of his life, as evidenced by many of his personal letters to friends. For example, he wrote: "I must despise a world that does not know that music is a higher revelation than all wisdom and philosophy. It is the wine which inspires one to new generative processes, and I am the Bacchus who presses out this glorious wine for mankind and makes them spiritually drunken . . . Well I know that God is nearer to me than to other artists. I associate with Him without fear. I have always recognized and understood Him and have no fear for my music — it can meet no evil fate. Those who understood it must be freed by it from all the miseries which the others drag about with themselves. . . . Music is the one incorporeal entrance into the higher world of knowledge which comprehends mankind but which mankind cannot comprehend."

It is natural for the inspired Sagittarian to be lifted above and beyond normal sense perception and to go into transports of ecstasy. Such were the experiences of Beethoven, which he once recounted as follows: "Incited by moods which are translated by the poet into words, by me into tones that sound and roar and storm about me until I have set them down in notes."

According to a mystic aphorism, "Before the feet can stand in the presence of the Master they must be washed in the blood of the heart." Beethoven knew from experience the profound truth of this statement. From early childhood sorrow accompanied him. His father was shiftless, improvident and an habitual drunkard whose chief interest in his son was to exploit his budding genius for personal ends. His mother, who died while Ludwig was still in his teens, placed upon him the care and responsibility of two younger brothers. It was with prophetic insight that he once declared he must live out his life alone. And so he did. His favorite brother, upon whom he lavished care and devotion, repaid him with callous indifference; his unworthy marriage proved to be a source of constant sorrow to Beethoven. After this brother's death Beethoven looked to his nephew Carl for consolation and companionship. Here again he met with complete lack of sympathy and understanding, along with utter ingratitude as well. Thus he was consistently denied the satisfaction of those close personal relations that every person longs for and that the great majority enjoy in greater or lesser measure.

The underlying reason for all this is clear. Beethoven's mission to earth lay in his music, so the Guardian of his destiny made sure no personal involvements would interfere with the fulfillment of that mission. Beethoven wrote that his life was ordained for high purpose and notable accomplishment. So it was. After he was mellowed by suffering and strengthened by the processes of detachment, his music assumed an heroic mould. In its profound immensities and magnificent proportions, it sang of the glories of other worlds and of higher states of being. No one can follow understandingly the transcendent strains of the *Eroica,* the *Third Symphony,* without realizing that in it he is sounding the triumphant chant of a life victorious. In the splendor of his symphonies he has traced steps whereby man progressively awakens to his divine destiny and rises majestically over his lesser self to a place of mastery.

As in the life of the Christ, the universal Way-shower, so in the life of the disciple who attains to Initiation or an illumined life. Gethsemane and Golgotha are followed by the Resurrection. This is the experience that Beethoven has transcribed in the triumphant chords of the *Eroica.* Each of his nine symphonies depicts some aspect of the great overcoming. So with the *Ninth,* the Symphony of Consummation. Beethoven was climbing his ladder of spiritual experience when he declared upon the completion of the *Seventh* that he felt his soul had risen to "heights in peace to serve Him."

As the composer's deafness increased with the years it tended to isolate him more and more from human intercourse; but it also seemed to lift him into high realms where he drew divine inspiration for his final works. His *Ninth Symphony* is a transcript of the soul-transport he experienced on those lofty levels. Here are his own words, which he had framed and then placed them on his desk: "I am that which is, I am all that was, that is and that shall be." The first three movements of his colossal *Ninth* depict the passage of the ascending spirit through the three heavens. In the final choral movement sounds the exaltation theme which sweeps the soul into the very presence of God. The symphony as a whole gives expression to the supreme realization that all life is one and immortal.

After this supernal work was finished, Beethoven's earthly mission was completed. His soul was set free to enter spheres where sound celestial symphonies of which his musical creations were, even at their best, but faint echoes. It is of these spheres that he sings in his final compositions. The *A Minor,* the *B Flat Major* and the *C Minor Concertos* reach the heights of transcendent consciousness and bridge ethereal spaces between earth and heaven.

Throughout his life Beethoven suffered deep and unending sorrow. It was the transmutation of this sorrow into positive spiritual values that crowned him as an immortal of his glorious art. On the last night of his earthly sojourn the heavens seemed to reflect his stormy years. The elements were troubled. Lightning flashed, thunder rolled as though all nature were sounding forth the strains Beethoven had incorporated in his *Appassionata Sonata.* As a final gesture he lifted his hand in eager salute to the seething elements. Then the great spirit was free to soar into those celestial spheres from which he had borrowed to produce music to uplift the children of earth.

Beethoven's color-tone was a deep Jupiterian purple-blue, and the purpose of his compositions is to aid in the development of cosmic consciousness.

*Chapter X*

## CAPRICORN—The Archangels

THE CONSTELLATION Capricorn is presumed to bear a resemblance to a goat. This, however, is not plainly discernible. In common with several other constellations, Capricorn does not possess any important stars, although across the head of the goat there are three comparatively bright ones, while a few others are sparsely scattered throughout its body.

Capricorn is the sign wherein occurs the Holy Nativity. Hence it may seem somewhat incongruous that a sign having such high spiritual qualifications should be designated as a goat. Then, when we turn to ancient Hebrew we find that the word which means *goat* also refers to the waters of eternal life. In this dual definition we discover an added meaning to King Solomon's song where he compares the hair of his beloved to a "flock of goats." When we understand that the "beloved" refers to the divinity within one's self, the meaning becomes much clearer.

The very oldest depictions of Capricorn show only the fore part of the symbol as a goat, the hind part being that of a fish. In the symbology of the ancients a fish always referred to something hidden or secret, especially the occult or esoteric. It was for this reason that the early Christians used fish as their signature. So we may perceive that the strange figure, half goat and half fish, bears a profound spiritual significance in harmony with the spiritual power of the sign Capricorn.

The Hierarchy of Capricorn is that of the Archangels. These high celestial Beings are expert manipulators of desire substance, and they contact this planet through the desire or astral realms. They work with both the human and animal kingdoms, teaching their natives how to build and use their desire bodies. The more advanced humanity of the present time is being taught how to refine and sublimate this body so that it will become increasingly responsive to spirit.

The supreme mission of the archangelic Host is to cleanse the astral realm of the dark, miasmic effluvium created by man's thoughts, words and deeds. This labor of purification is under the guidance of the four highest Archangels, those next to the Lord Christ in power and glory. From the Autumn Equinox, September 23rd, to the Winter Solstice, about December 22nd, this work is under the guidance of Michael and his ministering Hosts. From the Winter Solstice to the Spring Equinox, March 21st, this accomplishment is under the command of the beautiful Gabriel. From the Spring Equinox to the Summer Solstice, about June 22nd, it is directed by the holy Raphael. From the Summer Solstice to the Autumn Equinox, the sublime Uriel has charge of the work. This Herculean task of purification is the high planetary mission of the Archangels to the entire human race.

The universe we know is a mighty cosmic harp whose twelve zodiacal strings resound with the continuous Song of God. Each constellation vibrates its own keynote, and the majestic ensemble creates the *Music of the Spheres*. This music changes each month as the Sun passes from sign to sign. Nature responds in complete harmony with the cosmic symphony, consequently beauty and harmony are fundamental to her existence.

The ancients, instructed in their Mystery Temples regarding these truths, were sufficiently sensitized to attune themselves to the varying rhythms and thus developed symmetry and beauty of form, vibrancy of mind, and a longevity entirely unknown to us in this materialistic age. Now that we are on the threshold of the Aquarian Age, musical therapy based on stellar science is rapidly coming to the fore.

Capricorn is a month of profound mystery and tremendous possibilities. The Sun's entrance into this sign marks the wonder night of the year, the night when darkness is transformed into radiant light. It also inaugurates a season of introspection and recapitulation, inspiring seriousness and conducive to greater depths of meditation.

The musical keynote of Capricorn is G major. An ego finds innermost accentuation of his life's work in the musical rhythms of that zodiacal sign which open the door for its physical incarnation. Also, as previously noted, the Hierarchy of Libra gave to man the initial germ of his desire body. The Hierarchy of Capricorn is working to perfect that body. Therefore, the Capricorn native should receive much benefit and inspiration from musical compositions written in the keynotes of Libra, D major, and of Capricorn, G major.

During the season of the Holy Nativity one can receive much spiritual inspiration and soul exaltation from Christmas music. Previous mention has been made in this volume of the spiritual influence of such music. It is of enduring worth and will continue to live as long as the planet exists. This is particularly true of the *Ave Marias,* especially the one by Schubert. While hearing this music during Holy Season, those sufficiently sensitized will become conscious of a rare fragrance that always accompanies the love and blessing poured out by the Divine Virgin. During this season it is extremely potent, for the Blessed Lady and her ministering Angels are in close attendance upon the children of earth.

### CHARLES WAKEFIELD CADMAN — 1881-1946

Charles Wakefield Cadman is a well known Capricorn composer whose name is beloved wherever his music is heard. Born in Johnstown, Pennsylvania, December 24th, 1881, this brave pioneering spirit turned to his life work early in his youth when he first visited the Omaha Indian Reservation. Indian music was his forte; with it he did his best and most brilliant work. He wrote several Indian songs, among which *Land of the Sky Blue Water* is probably the best known.

Cadman also composed an Indian opera, *Shanewis* or *The Robin Woman,* that was produced by the Metropolitan Opera

Company in New York City and later in Hollywood Bowl. He travelled as a lecturer-recitalist for a number of years, accompanied by an Indian mezzo-soprano, Princess Trianina Red-Feather, and lectured in London and Paris on American Indian music.

Music is a recapitulation of human experience recorded in sound. Among Indian tribes the singer of historical narratives was second in distinction to the chief only. Their music retains something of the magic of Atlantis that was brought over by the Incas to the new Aryan continent. Its soothing harmonies are quite perceptible in Cadman's compositions.

It is significant to note that Capricorn is an earth sign and that American Indians are children of earth in a very special sense, being closely attuned to nature. Nature's color is green, and green is the color-tone in which this Capricorn native did his creative work. His deeply esoteric knowledge of both philosophy and life was incorporated into his compositions.

The termination of his earthly pilgrimage occurred in Hollywood, California, in the autumn of 1946, and was mourned by music lovers everywhere. His Indian music has been recognized as carrying marked physical benefit and as being especially effective in soothing tired, over-wrough nerves, particularly in instances of prolonged insomnia.

## GIACOMO PUCCINI — 1858-1924

Music of another Capricornian composer, Giacomo Puccini, is considered for its psychological effects. The works of this composer have been found effectual for meditative purposes. For example, if difficulty is experienced in closing out the objective world, making the mind one pointed as it were, esoteric students have been assisted in entering the silence by the beautiful aria *One Fine Day* from *Madam Butterfly*. It can lift one easily and quickly into the rarer atmosphere of spiritual realms wherein one's mind finds its true home. And Puccini's music is excellent for purposes of mental stimulation, retrospection and recapitulation — all of which are splended exercises for memory training.

Giacomo Puccini was born in Lucca, Italy, December 22nd, 1858. His whole family was musical. His father was an organist, and Giacomo commenced to compose for the organ at the age of nineteen. Through the influence of the Queen of Italy, he entered the Milan Conservatory in 1880, where he came under the tutelage of Ponchielli who soon recognized his youthful pupil's real talent.

Puccini's disposition was lovable and gentle, but he always bore the air of tender melancholy, a characteristic of Capricorn and the signature of its ruling planet Saturn. This melancholy note prodominates in his best known and most popular operas, *Manon Lescaut, La Boheme, La Tosca* and *Madam Butterfly*. The retrospective themes of these operas give evidence of the inspiration that Puccini found in Wagner. The love duet between Manon and Des Grieux in the second act of *Manon Lescault* evokes recollections of *Tristan and Isolde* in its high reaches of passion and pathos.

*Madam Butterfly* begins with a sort of tonal fugue representative of the ancient Japanese musical modes, which were never committed to writing but were passed from father to son among members of a sacred guild or musical hierarchy. Puccini said that the theme haunted him always, that it was constantly ringing in his head. Notwithstanding the abject failure of the opera's first performance and the crushing humiliation this brought to the composer, it is now considered by many critics as the most popular opera in the world today. Here again we note that the fortunes of Capricorn natives often swing from the depths to the heights.

Puccini was born on the cusp of Sagittarius and Capricorn, so drew idealism from the former and a sense of mystery from the latter. In *La Tosca* his skill has lifted crude melodrama into divine art. The third act of this opera is a magnificent mood-painting of night shadows which enshroud the prison of San Angelo as the ghost of the murdered Scarpio hovers near seeking vengeance. It is true Capricornian music, filled with the beauty and mystery of deeps profound and unexplored.

An early death in 1924 cut short Puccini's brilliant career. At the time of transition he was working on *Turandot,* an opera that gave promise of being his masterpiece. In it he changed from the tempo of the old age (Saturn in Capricorn) to the tempo of the new age (Uranus in Capricorn). Like Scriabin, he was experimenting with musical expressions that would release a greater measure of those creative impulses that are entering the human arena and consciousness at this time, and which both composers perceived as tending toward a new synthesis in our mundane and universal spheres.

The theme of this uncompleted opera was a simple human story; but the commonplace events dealt with were so sublimated by his genius that they assumed a deep significance. Ability to do this is another of Capricorn's gifts.

Students and lovers of New Age music felt they suffered an irreparable loss in the death of Puccini, which took place in Brussels. At the moment of his passing his fingers began to move lingeringly over the coverlet as though it were a piano. His face lightened as he seemed to be listening. Who could disbelieve that, as his hearing expanded to catch the harmonies of higher planes, he heard Angels singing the unfinished strains of his last and greatest opera, *Turandot?*

Puccini's color note is a deep clear pink with violet overtones. This is a color indicative of the sorrow and sufferings of a tragic love such as that depicted in two of his most popular operas – *La Boheme* and *Madame Butterfly.*

*Chapter XI*

## AQUARIUS—The Angels

AQUARIUS IS DEPICTED as a youth holding a water jug or similar vessel, from which he pours its contents into the starry river encircling his feet. The ancients identified this river as the sacred waters of heaven. Varied are the many picturizations of Aquarius. Often the youth bears in his hands two cups, pouring water from one onto the sea, from the other onto the land; and where the land touches the sea mysterious flowers have sprung into life. Hence, he pours out the water of immortality, of which the new Aquarian race shall partake. It is the same water that the Christ gave to the woman by the well in Samaria, telling her that when she drank of it she would never again thirst. The youthful figure of Aquarius was looked upon by the ancients as the cupbearer who brought the water of immortality to the gods.

The starry script of the heavens contains much prophecy pertaining to the approaching Aquarian Age. One of the heavenly dome's brightest lights is Altair in the constellation of Aquila, the Eagle. An eagle is ever a symbol of the spiritual attainment belonging to Aquaria. Nearby is Lyra, the Harp. This constellation is the home of magnificent Vega whose brilliance illumines the sky. This star has been regarded with wonder and reverence by star worshipers of all ages, and in times long past it was the pole star of our planet. In a future age it will become so again. When this occurs the power and magic of music will be fully comprehended, and man will live, move and have his being in a divine harmony unknown to him today.

Another prophetic constellation is Cygnus, the Swan. Its brightest stars form the glittering Northern Cross. Both the cross and the swan are significant symbols of Initiation, the former representing Initiation into the Christian Mysteries; the latter, Initiation into the medieval Mysteries, as illustrated by Wagner's *Lohengrin*. This music-drama is not an impossible fairy story; rather, it recounts a most beautiful phase of Initiation belonging to the Medieval Age.

In the coming Aquarian Age Initiation will be the foundation stone of New Age religion. The following stirring lines by Edwin Markham sound the challenge call of Aquaria:

*Come, clear the way, then, clear the way*
*Blind creeds and kings have had their day.*
*Break the dead branches from the path:*
*Our hope is in the aftermath —*
*Our hope is in heroic men,*
*Star-led to build the world again.*
*To this event the ages ran:*
*Make way for Brotherhood — make way for man.*

The same freedom song of the New Age characterizes music centered in the rhythmic currents of Aquarius, sign of the Waterbearer.

Since the life and works of every ego bear the zodiacal impress of its nativity sign, composers born under this stellar signature have sung unvaryingly of freedom, emancipation and equality. Their music seems to have been wafted from the far spaces, and it breathes of pure air in happier climes.

Aquarius is a sign of vision. Under its influence man is truly star-led and star-guided. The impulses of Aquarius enable one's spirit to mount with ever increasing fervor toward a chosen goal, undaunted by what may appear to be insurmountable difficulties. A new horizon beckons enticingly and one's life is animated by the sole purpose of union with New Age rhythms. The Aquarian spirit is untrammelled. It chafes at boundaries. Its soul sings with the poet:

*Each age is a dream that is dying —*
*For one that is coming to birth.*

## AQUARIUS—*The Angels*

The Hierarchy of Aquarius is that of the Angels, who contact earth by way of the etheric realms. They are expert manipulators of etheric substance and assist in the fashioning of etheric bodies for natives of the human, animal and plant kingdoms. This accounts for their not being visible to ordinary sight. As soon as one develops clairvoyance (clearsight) he is able to observe their nearness and the many phases of their lovely ministrations to every living thing upon the earth planet. They are now working to aid pioneers of the next race in the building of soul-bodies, that Golden Wedding Garment fashioned of the higher ethers. Those who will meet the Christ in the etheric realms must, through spiritual living, weave this radiant soul-garment so they will be able to work with Him in establishing His new kingdom.

The musical keynote of Aquarius is A major. As has been previously stated, the initial impulse of the etheric body was given to humanity by the Hierarchy of Virgo. It is now being finished by the Hierarchy of Aquarius, the Angels. So musical compositions written in the keynote of Virgo, C natural, and of Aquarius, A major, should prove both stimulating and illuminating to an Aquarian native.

The music of Mozart is recommended for mental alertness. If one desires to develop one-pointedness of mind, the ability to concentrate upon a single subject for a stipulated period of time, he should practice exercises for this to the accompaniment of Mozart's music, preferably his symphonies. If one has children who are irritable and fractious, use the fairy music of Mendelssohn, such as that from *Midsummer Night's Dream* and his *Songs Without Words*. Do not oblige a child to listen to the music, just play it softly and note the result. For spiritual meditation use Schubert's beautiful songs and his *Ave Maria*.

Cyril Scott is a well known composer and the author of *Music, Its Secret Influence throughout the Ages,* a most illuminating treatise on esoteric music. He states that, as we enter the Aquarian Age, and in consideration of the tremendous influence of music in the formation of character, he believes that the spiritual Hierarchies will be instrumental in giving to the world an international hymn. This will not be of a type that stresses the superiority of one nation above another, but it will tend to bring them all into one vast brotherhood and thus establish unity out of diversity.

The existing music which most nearly coincides with this universal ideal is the concluding Choral from Beethoven's *Ninth Symphony*. In its great up-sweep of ecstatic joy and soul exaltation, it sounds the universal note of harmony, unity, peace and brotherhood. In it is heard the sublime chant intoning the Oneness of All and the Allness of One, the ideal of every true son of Aquaria.

## Franz Schubert — 1797-1828

Prominent upon the roster of Aquarian musicians is Franz Schubert. True to his stellar signature, the most noteworthy fact connected with his personal life was his great devotion to his friends. Many of his loveliest songs, as well as much of his piano music, owed their inspiration to the happy hours of companionship spent with those he loved. They were so large a part of his life that in every biography of this composer much space and importance are alloted to these friends whose influence upon his life was secondary only to his music.

Schubert was born January 31st, 1797, in Lichtenthal, a suburb of Vienna, and he remained his entire life in or near this city. He wove its beauty, rhythm and harmony into the very soul of his music, which caused his closest friends to give him the title of the "Vienna nightingale."

Again in accordance with his Aquarian characteristics, Schubert has been described as a man of the people, one who could both work and play with them and then create beautiful music as a result of his warm humanitarianism.

At the tender age of thirteen the impulse to compose swept over him so powerfully that the impediments of poverty, stern parental disapproval and lack of training failed to deter him. His divine godhood demanded musical expression. He had come to earth to sing, and sing he must and would despite all obstacles.

In astrological parlance Aquarius is termed an airy sign. This means that if they so will, its natives may develop ethereal qualities; that is, in mind and spirit they may soar beyond the limitations of time and space. They possess the ability to rise above an environment of limitation and to create for themselves a new world teeming with possibilities inherent in the coming Aquarian day.

The soul of Franz Schubert found refuge from the sordidness of his objective environment in the etheric beauty of this higher realm. Later, in the language of music, he described it as few composers have been able to do. Biographical references have been made to the "Spiritual Island" wherein his soul abided in ecstatic recognition of that which is timeless and spaceless. Inspiration from this source found expression more than six hundred songs, eight of which Schubert composed in one day. So prodigal was he in scattering his rare treasures that a final assembling for publication of his works required more years than the span of his earth life. He died in 1828 at the age of thirty-one.

Schubert was deeply attached to a song he dedicated to the Blessed Virgin. In his lovely *Ave Maria* he touched the keynote of the Divine Lady, which accounts for the magic healing power of its music.

It was natural that Schubert, a son of air, should have a particular fondness for sylphs. These diminutive and translucent creatures were his favorite nature spirits. Much of his music possesses their ethereal and elfin quality. In his wanderings he often listened to their eerie songs and then transcribed them to what have become immortal notes.

Besides his songs there is all the lovely chamber music, in the writing of which he excelled, and piano pieces without number. Like Beethoven, however, symphonies were his crowning product. Who can listen to his sublime *Symphony in B Minor* without realizing that he is singing of celestial sights and scenes that transcend even his noble genius? Hence, his *Unfinished Symphony*.

Schubert's color note is rose-lavender, correlated to the love nature attuned to sorrow. In his music will be found a panacea for the stabilization of one's emotions. He described himself as "being always torn between love and pain." Music was for him a soul remedy for this conflicting alternation. Upon its ecstatic rhythms he was able to attune himself to that great center wherein abideth the peace that passeth understanding.

## Wolfgang Mozart — 1756-1791

Wolfgang Mozart first came into the light of day in Salzburg, Austria, on January 27th, 1756. The father of the infant held a position as court composer and leader of the court orchestra under Archbishop Sigismund. One of Mozart's earliest musical memories was of hearing a band stationed on the walls of the city and playing his father's composition entitled *The Morning and Evening Melodiously and Harmoniously Introduced to the Inhabitants of Salzburg*. This shows how music was more closely and intimately a part of people's lives at that time than it is now.

Mozart was endowed with rich and golden gifts for his destined work. At four years of age he became inwardly aware of his mission as a master musician through the ecstasy which possessed him while listening to the song of a feathered chorister. Immediately thereafter he began to play, astounding everyone who heard him by his marvelous talent. Obsessed by the true rhythms of Aquarius, the child was not content merely to interpret the words of other composers. His was an impelling urge to become a channel whereby new and hitherto uncreated harmonies might be brought into audibility. Another endowment was his amazing memory. After having attended a Good Friday service at St. Peters in Rome where he heard the famous *Miserere* (Allegris), he wrote out the entire composition from memory . When it was compared with the original it was found to be letter perfect.

This spirit, so animated by divine fire, remained upon earth only a brief thirty-five years, and yet how glorious is the heritage of beauty and worth that he bequeathed to man! The final ten years of his life, spent in Vienna, were the most barren and physically wretched. Still, they produced the most gloriously fruitful expression of his creative genius. They were the years that brought forth *Don Giovanni, The Magic Flute* and his *Requiem Mass;* also the magnificent *Jupiter Symphony,* a glorious climax to his artistry in musical composition and to his indomitable spirit. This great symphony proclaims the complete triumph of spirit over all the ills and limitations of mortality.

Mozart passed his youth in the Roman Catholic faith. On reaching manhood he became an equally devout Mason. The theme of the *Magic Flute* is centered in the esotericism of Masonic ritual. Thus, as a pioneer genius, he labored at the foot of the two columns of Fire and Water, the elements upon which the evolution of all mankind is based. Musically, he expressed this union in the perfect blending of form and feeling.

During the evening hours of December 4th, 1791, Mozart's last upon earth, he rehearsed with a group of friends his *Requiem,* which he called his death song. As December 5th dawned he asked to hear the music of *The Magic Flute.* To its beloved strains his spirit slipped away to enter those bright realms where music is all-pervading and eternal.

## FELIX MENDELSSOHN — 1809-1847

It is natural that children of Aquarius manifest their talents early in life. This was true of Felix Mendelssohn, who gave his first public concert at the age of nine and had begun setting down his own musical compositions before that. Again, true to the Aquarian type, he possessed many gifts in addition to his musical genius. Prior to his teens he was an honored guest of Goethe at Weimar. It was said of him that "he paints, writes verse, is proficient in Greek and Latin, and is quite nimble in athletics."

Light, movement, beauty, color! These were keywords of Mendelssohn's life as they are of his music. His *Midsummer Night's Dream* score is largely descriptive of his own experience. Reared in a home of wealth and luxury, we find him as a lad of seventeen lightly reading aloud to a group of youthful companions the first German translation of Shakespeare's fairy play. The beautiful gardens of his father's palatial estate are the setting for this reading, a locale as lovely as that of the fantasy itself. Amid these same beautiful surroundings he later wrote the Overture for it.

From childhood his etheric vision delighted in the tiny creatures that frolic and dance with merry abandon just beyond the borderline of physical sight. It was completely natural, therefore, that tripping elves and airy sprites should revel in his compositions; and that this son of air should give us music which bears his soul's signature and may be classed among the world's most delightful and truly descriptive fairy harmonies. While a mere toddler Felix would frequently wave his little cap to his mother and sister with the salutation "I'm off to see the Queen" or "I am going to Fairyland." This unquenchable spirit of youth remained with him always. Seventeen years after the Overture was written he added the *Schertzo* and *Wedding March,* both in the same delightful vein.

Mendelssohn exhibited the most miraculous memory, also typical of Aquarius. While still a mere child he would sit at the piano for hours and play from memory compositions of masters such as Bach, Beethoven and Mozart. His clairvoyant faculties enabled him to be in touch with each one of them to such an extent that even his features changed into a likeness of the composer whose work he was interpreting. A further evidence of his extraordinary memory was his ability to construct an improvisation on numbers he heard at a concert, employing every theme, instrumental or vocal, to which he had listened.

Aquarius has two rulers: Uranus which heralds the *new* and Saturn which adheres to the *old.* Mozart typifies the Uranus-Aquarian while Mendelssohn represents the Saturn-

Aquarian. The later vehemently denounced the idea of "new music." "New roads indeed! The artist is but led astray who gives himself up to the cursed demon!" he asserted, "It is not new culture which we behold in the advance, it is only the old made more exquisite, more perfect." His Aquarian perception sensed the wonder of New Age Music but his Saturnian heritage prevented him from participating in its perpetuation.

The color-tone of Mendelssohn is a clear, pure pink so typical of the brightness, gayety and harmony that conditioned his life. His music may be used for developing etheric or extended vision.

Consistent with his life pattern, Mendelssohn's passing was one of peace and beauty. Death laid a serene impress upon his always handsome features. Surrounded by the homage and acclaim so familiar to him, this bright spirit attained final release to the appropriate accompaniment of his own *Song without Words.*

Chapter XII

## PISCES—Virgin Spirits

THE SYMBOL for the constellation of Pisces is composed of two fishes bound together by a cord but swimming in opposite directions. In the mouth of each fish is a star, one of these being Fomalhaut, a brilliant star of the first magnitude.

To repeat, in all symbolical language *fish* typify that which is hidden, secret, occult. Disciples of the Lord Christ used this symbol as their signature because they were students of the secret Mysteries of early Christianity. The *sea* stands for the psychic realms, the mystic deeps of which have been penetrated only by the greatest Masters. This symbology explains why the Lord's teachings contain so many references to the sea, to fishermen and to fish. He was instructing His chosen Disciples regarding inner mysteries pertaining to psychic realms.

Pisces is the home of some of the Zodiac's most profound secrets. It governs the oceans of the physical plane, those vast and little explored depths that are as yet intangible and indefinable. In the field of consciousness Pisces rules the aspect of universality. Its element is water. In man its vehicle of expression is his emotional nature in the lower triad of personality; his spiritual nature in the higher trinity of egoic being. Pisces calls to the deeps in man and is disposed to arouse emotional upheavals comparable to the restless rolling of the ocean. The sign is ruled by the great benefic Jupiter and by Neptune, planet of divinity. Also, it is the exaltation place of Venus.

Pisces natives are illusive, mystical and imaginative. Their greatest power is focused in the realm of the unseen, the unseen to which all are related by higher vehicles. Depending on his spiritual development, a Piscean may be a mere self-centered dreamer or a person of vision dedicated in service to mankind.

That there have been many of the latter type is attested by any nation's Hall of Fame, for among its notables there is always a preponderance of Piscean sons.

Pisces is also a sign of karma or ripe destiny, of reaping what has been sown in the past, since it closes a cycle of experience.

As already said, the Lords of Leo (A sharp major) awakened the divine spirit within early humanity, while the Lords of Sagittarius (F major) bestowed upon it the link of mind. The spiritual keynote of Pisces (B major) is in the image and likeness of God. It makes for the perfecting of the physical body, spiritualizing the Sagittarian mind, and bringing the forces of body and mind under the dominion of spirit under Leo, thus completing the work of the great zodiacal life cycle. All musical compositions in the keynotes of Leo, Sagittarius and Pisces are stimulating, inspiring and illuminating to the native Piscean.

The Hierarchy of Aries holds the Cosmic Pattern of perfected man. The ideal of Pisces is attainment of this perfection. Throughout an ego's life cycles under the successive zodiacal signs, each Hierarchy aids its progress and development toward such perfection.

The Bible, the supreme textbook of humanity, opens with the creative fiat that man be made in the image and likeness of God, this fiat being given in the Book of Genesis. The Book of Revelation concludes with the sublime vision of the hundred and forty-four (1 plus 4 plus 4 or 9, the number of humanity) thousand emancipated Beings standing upon a sea of glass (etheric realms), robed in white and bearing upon their foreheads the mark of the Christ. This describes man's perfected physical body together with a Christed mind in complete unity with divine spirit, the exalted attainment awaiting the race.

### FREDERIC CHOPIN — 1809-1849

The celebrated French-Polish composer, Frederic Chopin, was born in March, 1809. His characteristics, temperament, ideals, aims and purposes were so completely in accord with his birth sign that to study one is to study the other. In other words, Chopin was in all respects a typical Piscean. Corroborating this statement is the following description by Franz Liszt, his devoted friend and fellow artist: "He kept apart from all noisy and frequented ways and built a secluded cell for himself. As the devout pour out their souls in prayer, so he poured his soul into his compositions. What others say on their knees, he uttered in tone-language – all the mysteries of passion and grief which man can understand without words, because there are no words in which they can adequately be expressed."

Chopin was friendly and generous, ever ready to extend a helping hand where needed. Yet he possessed a pronounced inner reserve, an aloofness that not even his closest intimates were ever able to completely dispel.

Liszt tells us that Chopin, true to the water nature of his zodiacal ruler, wished all of his compositions played with a rocking, undulatory motion simulating the rippling movement of water. "By his peculiar style of playing," Liszt wrote, "Chopin imparted with most fascinating effect this constant rocking, causing the melody to undulate to and fro like a skiff driven over the bosom of tossing waves. This manner of execution, which set so peculiar a seal upon his style of performance, he indicated by affixing to his works the words *tempo rubato,* meaning a tempo broken, agitated, interrupted."

Chopin's color-note, an exquisite azure blue, denoted in the language of color symbology "spirit's compensation for sorrow." A Piscean is highly sensitive to the inflow of spiritual impulses in times of stress and grief. Since such impulses flowed into Chopin's compositions, they are literal healing agencies for those passing through such times. Liszt intuitively associated Chopin with azure . Writing about the latter's music, he refers to "depths of etherean and spiritual azure," and compares the composer's person to "a convolvulus balancing its azure-hued cup upon a very slight stem, the tissue of which is so vaporous that the slightest contact wounds and tears its delicate corolla."

Venus, planet of personal love, is, we have said, exalted in Pisces, sign of sorrow. Through personal love man experiences his Gethsemane, and in his travail his inner depths are quickened. The strength drawn therefrom makes his resurrection possible. Chopin knew well the meaning of the agony garden. He also knew the calm that is victorious over turmoil, the peace that triumphs over pain. All this he imparted to his immortal music; and this it is which gives to his music that indefinable sadness so characteristic of all his compositions. Even his gayest musical moments appear to be the result of laughter disguising a heart in tears.

George Sand, the famous French novelist, referred to Chopin as the "lover of an Impossible so shadowy and so near the stellar regions." She stated that his music "bears her on rapid wings to scenes which are impossible to describe but which must exist in this world or on some of the planets whose light we love to contemplate in the forest when the moon has set." Writing about him and his music, this author naturally fell into a Neptunian-Piscean style, employing qualities belonging to the supernal and to things mystical.

Chopin passed in 1849 at a mere forty years of age. As his earthly remains lay almost buried in roses, his ethereal beauty — the gift of Venus exalted in Pisces — was even more pronounced than during his life. Parisian artists and devotees of all that is lovely turned out *en massé* for the last rites, administered to the accompaniment of Mozart's *Requiem* and to the strains of the composer's own *Funeral March,* then played for the first time.

To catch the spirit of beauty was the goal of Chopin's earthly journey and quest. It was also his immortal heritage as a child of Pisces, and he passed this heritage on to all mankind in his exquisite music.

## Georg Friedric Handel — 1685-1759

Handel was born February 23rd, 1685, in Halle, Saxony. Scarcely noted in this quiet hamlet was the birth of a child destined to become one of the world's greatest composers, one whose music has exerted a widespread spiritual benefit to a degree little realized by even music lovers. He came with a high mission and that mission he fulfilled in a most glorious manner.

From early childhood Handel had but a single ambition, and that was to be a musician. It was his one all-absorbing interest. The toys in his nursery were chiefly flutes, trumpets and drums. But this preoccupation was so greatly disliked by his father that he forbade his son to have any of it in the home. Moreover, Handel Sr. did not allow his budding genius to attend schools where music was part of the required curriculum.

Born as he was on the cusp of Aquarius and Pisces, young Georg Friederic had ability and determination for overcoming these great obstacles. The mysticism of Pisces augmented the vision of Aquarius, giving him a mystic vision that guided him, undeterred and undismayed, toward the brilliant fulfillment of his destined career. For instance, when he was only seven he contrived to slip a small clavichord into his garret room. During the night, while his father was asleep, he taught himself to play the instrument. Eventually, realizing his inability to stem the musical aspirations of his son, the senior Handel permitted the boy to study the organ, with the result that, at the age of eleven Handel was composing fugues and cantatas almost without number. Working indefatigably under the high inspiration of his calling, Handel also learned to play the harpsichord, violin and oboe.

Handel became organist for the Halle Cathedral and, later, held the same position in Hamburg. There he wrote his first *Passion,* which was performed during Holy Week of 1704.

In those days Italy was the goal of all musicians. It was there Handel formed a close friendship with the noted Scarlatti, one of the finest harpsichord players of his day. No professional jealously could keep them apart because Handel was of a generous, magnanimous spirit that soared above all petty rivalries. Music was to him a divine art. He held that as such it should be used only for man's ennoblement. True to this ideal, he dedicated his life to composing and performing such music exclusively as would serve to inspire and beautify the lives of others.

Handel's most fruitful and satisfying years were spent in England. It was there that friends, favor and fortune sought him out; and it was there he had the transcendent musical experience of writing his most celebrated oratorio, *The Messiah*. During this sublime period the very gates of heaven were open to him, and he was lifted up in ecstatic vision to see and hear the celestial chorusing of Angels. Recounting his transport, Handel declared, "I think I did see all Heaven before me and the great God Himself."

Music critics consider *The Messiah* as one of the greatest masterpieces ever composed. It was completed in twenty-two days, and was accomplished during his own crucifixion in a garden where he was hounded by creditors, enemies, defamatory reports and lies. His personal career appeared to be well nigh ended. The Agony Rite in the Garden is placed astronomically in the crypt of Pisces. Natives of this sign are all too often familiar with its significance. Handel, great soul that he was, transcended his personal trials and was raised to the very portals of heaven that he might transmit for human hearing the majestic grandeur of *The Messiah*. While he was engaged in this task tears of joy and gratitude mingled with the ink being used to transcribe its celestial music.

After finishing *The Messiah* Handel lived in ever closer attunement with higher realms. During his final illness he expressed a desire to leave this earth on Good Friday so as to meet his "sweet Lord and Saviour on the day of His resurrection." The wish was granted. At the mystic hour of midnight on the borderline between Good Friday and Holy Saturday, April 13th, 1759, Georg Friederic Handel passed into fellowship with angelic Hosts.

Handel's color-note is white-silver. His music may be used to bring about communion with Angels. The *Hallelujah Chorus* from *The Messiah* is particularly effective for establishing such contact.

## MAURICE RAVEL – 1875-1937

Maurice Ravel, the eminent French composer, was a foremost exponent of the music of tomorrow. True to his Piscean nature, he tended toward concealment. It was said of him that he "carried the proud reserve of all those who bear a message whose secret has not yet been revealed."

Early in life he became dedicated to music. He literally lived, moved and had his being in rhythm, as evidenced by his *Bolero* and *L'Heure Espagnole,* two of his best known works. As a child he was intuitively conscious of inner-plane activities and held close communion with the hidden world. Later, he wove his heard impressions into exquisite tone-poems.

Ravel's color-tone is a delicate green shot through with red and silver. His music may be used to advantage for developing inner sight.

We remarked in connection with Chopin that natives of water signs have a natural affinity for this element. Ravel described his inspiration as a musical hydrant, adding that music flowed from it without any effort on his part. He often referred to the inspiration given to him by water. One of his favorite piano pieces was *Jeaux d'eau,* a number scintillant with the sheen of rainbow fountains and rippling waterfalls. He said of his composition: "the fluvial God laughs at the water that tickles him."

## MODEST MOUSSORGSKY – 1839-1881

Modest Moussorgsky, who doubtless stands supreme among Russian moderns, was born March 16th, 1839. His mother's family were aristocrats, while his father's people were serfs on one side. Out of this blending came the understanding, compassion, love of the people and spirit of universalism that influenced the life and music of this extraordinary genius. Indicative of his wide sympathies are the words he wrote to friends: "It is the people I want to depict, sleeping, waking, eating, drinking. I hold them constantly in mind. Again and again they rise before me, huge, unvarnished, and with no tinsel trappings. An artist who digs deep enough will have cause for joy at the results."

Moreover, Moussorgsky said that he longed to know his people and to be admitted to their brotherhood. This he accomplished through his music, which so clearly depicts a new and brighter Russia that his compositions have been pin-pointed as the initial cause of the social unrest among the masses that eventuated in the revolution. He claimed further that his interest in the spirit of people and their mode of life were the chief incentive for his piano improvisations before he had learned the most rudimentary rules of music.

From childhood Moussorgsky was a sensitive and a mystic. He was deeply interested in such metaphysical topics as life after death, clairvoyance and communion between planes, subjects that are second nature to Piscean natives – although during his college and military years he attempted to disavow them and to profess atheism. In *Khovanstchina,* his last opera, and *Boris Godounov,* considered his greatest, he returned to the subject of religious mysticism. Both operas stress the liberty and free thinking of the people, privileges not granted them under czarist Russia any more than they are under Soviet totalitarianism.

Moussorgsky's younger years were steeped in the fairy lore that found exquisite expression in his musical poems of childhood. Toward the end of his life his musical interests were centered in a portrayal of the poetry of death, a mystical lore transcending all outer forms and becoming a link between the seen and the unseen, the physical and the spiritual. A friend described the composer's naive and childlike personality thus: "He was so innocent in the things of life that to him it was quite impossible that any educated and well-bred man could ever cause pain to his neighbor or ever play a dirty trick on him. He was an ideal personality."

Moussorgsky wielded a magic whereby the beautiful is evoked from the most forbidding forms, conditions and circumstances. His Piscean mysticism penetrated to the heart of things where he beheld their hidden peace and purpose. He sublimated the ugly and gave dignity to the commonplace. In this faculty lay his greatest strength, and it is the most distinguishing quality of his superb work. Also, it is this strength which gives his work its strange and discordant rhythms.

In time the art of transmutation will be incorporated in musical psychology as offered by university curriculums. Meditative exercises will form a part of such work and will be accompanied by the music of moderns like Moussorgsky, Shoenberg and Stravinsky, to name but three.

Moussorgsky was attuned to Neptune, ruler of Pisces and planet of divinity. This planet sounds the highest string of the human lyre and is, therefore, most easily "jangled out of tune" by the harsh events of mortal existence. The discord between man's fallen nature and his divine nature is heard in Moussorgsky's music — but not just the discords only, for it is charged with intense desire to surmount the pain they bring and to raise man to high soul-levels where concord alone prevails. This latter contributes the upbuilding, inspiring quality that pervades the ofttimes austere and terrible grandeur of this sensitive Piscean's music.

Thus his music expresses not only humanity's cry for release from painful bondage to its own unregenerate nature, but a cry for release from such bondage as he experienced in his own being. He knew himself to be one with humanity at large, part human and part divine. As a Piscean he was deeply aware of the higher side of his nature and like Hamlet, another Piscean in nature and outlook, he found it difficult to adjust himself to "this too, too solid flesh." The resulting tragedy was the same for one as it was for the other. In Moussorgsky's case, however, it led to excesses along Neptunian lines that terminated his life prematurely by uncontrolled dissipation.

The color-note of Moussorgsky is sea blue flecked with crimson, bespeaking an energetic devotion to the true and the beautiful. In one of his final utterances he proclaimed his credo as man and artist in these ringing sentences: "My battle-cry remains the same. Go boldly on! Forward to new shores and give yourself wholly to mankind – that is what art requires of you now!"

Hear, also, the Mystic Neptune speaking through him as he proclaims his faith in the future and his power to achieve it: "My task is clear, with ever greater eagerness I press forward to new shores in the shoreless sea of Art to seek new countries, never resting, never stopping, without fear or wavering, to set foot firmly on the ground of the Promised Land – that is the great and beautiful aim."

# CONCLUSION

This work on the Cosmic Harp opened with a statement relative to the power and magic of music, a statement made by Max Heindel, a leading occult scientist and a prominent expositor of Rosicrucian Philosophy.

We conclude it with a statement made by a musical scientist, Professor Donald Hatch Andrews of John Hopkins University, who has made many fascinating experiments in sound. He summarizes his conclusions as follows:

> *"All things in the universe, including you and me, are nothing more than a mass of vibrating waves. All we ever see is the outward shadow of the reality — the wave form. That is why it seems to me that the true values in the universe are spiritual values."*

Professor Andrews concludes:

> *"The more we try to pin down reality in electrons, the more it vanishes under our fingertips. The universe apparently is composed entirely of music. The human spirit is the ultimate reality of life on earth, and the spirit of the universe is the supreme reality."*

## BY THE SAME AUTHOR

### NEW AGE BIBLE INTERPRETATIONS

Six Volumes: Three on the O.T., three on the N.T.
Mystery of the Christos
Tarot and the Bible
Mythology and the Bible
Mystic Masonry and the Bible
Occult Anatomy and the Bible
Stellar Science and the Bible
Star Gates: the Solstices and Equinoxes
Science of Numbers and the Bible
Questions and Answers on Biblical Enigmas
Easter Mysteries
Christmas Mysteries
Supreme Initiations of the Blessed Virgin
Through the Year with Mary
Lenten Pearls
Twelve Steps That Lead to the Illumined Life
Magic Gardens: How the Angels say it with flowers

### COLOR AND MUSIC

Color and Music in the New Age
Music: the Keynote of Human Evolution
Healing and Regeneration through Color
Healing and Regeneration through Music
The Cosmic Harp
Wagner's Music Dramas Esoterically Interpreted
Beethoven's Nine Symphonies

## NEW AGE PRESS PUBLICATIONS

By Theodore Heline

*Studies in This Changing World*

AMERICA'S DESTINY —
A New Order of the Ages ..........

THE AMERICAN INDIAN —
Our Relations and Responsibilities ..........

FUNDAMENTAL FEATURES OF THE WORLD CRISIS

JAPAN —
Her Double Astrological Rulership
Aries-Libra; The Sword and the Cherry Blossom ..........

JAPAN —
A Semi-Westernized Orient ..........

POLAND —
The Land of the White Eagle ..........

TURKEY —
Lebanon and the Land of Araby ..........

ICELAND —
Home of the Ancient Benjamites—Fascinating Study ..........

Drama for Light on the Path

SHAKESPEARE —
Romeo and Juliet—The Law of Polarity ..........

SHAKESPEARE —
Merchant of Venice—Head vs Heart ..........

PEABODY —
The Wolf of Gubbio—St. Francis and the Wolf ..........

IBSEN —
Peer Gynt—The Redemptive Feminine ..........

MAETERLINCK —
The Blue Bird—Journey Into Truth ..........

CAPEK —
R. U. R.—As In the Days of Noah ..........

Other Studies

DEAD SEA SCROLLS —
Essenian Forerunners of Christ ..........

GANDHI —
The Prophet of Love in Action ..........

CAPITAL PUNISHMENT —
Historical Trends Toward Abolishment ..........

ARCHETYPE UNVEILED —
Study of Creative Word Sound Patterns ..........